FORT UNION TRADING POST
FUR TRADE EMPIRE ON THE UPPER MISSOURI

By
Erwin N. Thompson

1986
Theodore Roosevelt Nature and History Association
Medora, ND

Theodore Roosevelt Nature & History Association
P.O. Box 167
Medora, North Dakota 58645

Theodore Roosevelt Nature and History Association is a non-profit
organization dedicated to the preservation and interpretation of
the National Parks and National Historic Sites in North Dakota.

ISBN 0-9601652-2-3

First Printing, 1986
Second Printing, 1988

Contents

Acknowledgments

Several years ago, the National Park Service allowed me the privilege of preparing a "historic structure report" of Fort Union Trading Post. Now, the opportunity has come about to adapt that report to a history of the grand old post founded over 150 years ago. My thanks go to the past and present superintendents and staff of Theodore Roosevelt National Park and Fort Union Trading Post National Historic Site for continuing support. My appreciation goes, also, to my former supervisors and associates in the National Park Service who aided the project and, most of whom, like myself, are now retired.

To the many public and private institutions who made their historical resources available, my thanks to:

Detroit Public Library
Hudson's Bay Company, Winnipeg, Manitoba
Joslyn Art Museum, Omaha, Nebraska
Library of the Boston Athenaeum
Minnesota Historical Society
Missouri Historical Society
Montana Historical Society
Ontario Provincial Archives, Toronto
Public Archives of Canada, Ottawa
Royal Ontario Museum, Toronto
Smithsonian Institution, Washington, D.C.
St. Louis University Library, St. Louis
University of California at Los Angeles
Washington State University, Pullman
Wilder Library, Harvard College
Wisconsin Historical Society
Yale University Library

Gratitude is due to several museums and archives who provided illustrations and who are credited herein.

Introduction

Fort Union Trading Post, founded in 1829, was the grandest of the extensive network of fur posts erected on the upper Missouri and Yellowstone rivers by the American Fur Company and its rivals in the nineteenth century. This headquarters post, peopled by a succession of strong personalities and supplied via steamboats, became a proud citadel in the wilderness. Because of its significant role in the nation's history, Fort Union is a unit in the National Park System.

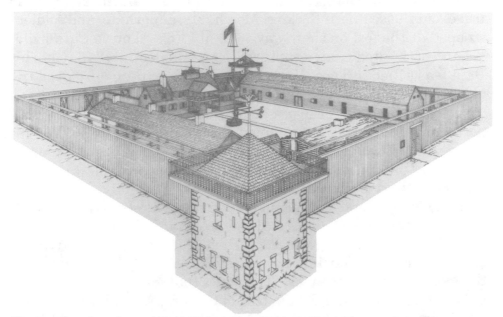

Perspective drawing of Fort Union based on the historical and archeological evidence, which was drawn by Paul Briggs, National Park Service, 1979. *Courtesy Fort Union Trading Post NHS.*

Four other fur trading establishments are also national historic sites. In Minnesota, Grand Portage, dating from the eighteenth century, commemorates the North West Company of Montreal, whose adventurers explored the breadth of North America to the Yukon and to the mouth of the Columbia. Each summer at Grand Portage, a great gathering occurred when the partners from the interior met with the gentlemen from Montreal in the Great Hall for business and high revelry. When the boundary between the United States and British possessions to the north was established in 1804, Grand Portage was abandoned.

In the far west, the Hudson's Bay Company constructed Fort Vancouver on the north bank of the Columbia River in present

Washington in 1824-25. From here, the mighty British company administered its realms that reached from Spanish California to Russian Alaska and eastward to the Rocky Mountains. When the western boundary settlement with Great Britain was achieved in 1846, the Hudson's Bay Company moved its Western Department headquarters north to Vancouver Island. Fort Vancouver eventually became a U.S. Army post.

In what is now southeastern Colorado, the St. Louis brothers Charles and William Bent, built a large adobe post on the Santa Fe Trail in 1833. Here, trappers and pathfinders outfitted for their travels in the southern Rockies. Merchants, emigrants, and soldiers stopped at the fort on their way to Santa Fe and on to California. When the United States captured New Mexico in 1846, Charles Bent was killed in Taos. His brother, William, then destroyed the old fort and rebuilt elsewhere.

On the Laramie River in present Wyoming, Rocky Mountain trappers built a fort that they named Fort William in 1834. Within a few years it was replaced by a more substantial structure named John. William or John, the establishment became known to history as Fort Laramie. Tens of thousands of emigrants on the trails to Oregon and California passed its gates. In 1849, the U.S. Army purchased the site, retaining the name Fort Laramie.

All five forts rank high in the history of the fur trade and in the exploration of the continent. Their stories are important pieces in the mosaic of the Great West. The pages that follow tell the history of Fort Union Trading Post, a tale of traders, Assiniboins, Crows, Blackfeet, artists, princes, steamboats, beaver, buffalo, and life on the upper Missouri over one hundred years ago.

CHAPTER 1

Men, Furs, and Empires

The upper Missouri did not quickly reveal its mysteries to the hunters and traders of the French colonies. For the century after two **Quebeçois**, Louis Jolliet, a **coeur de bois**, and Father Jacques Marquette, a Jesuit, discovered the river's mouth in 1673, geographers could but guess about the Missouri's headwaters. By the 1770s, however, British and Canadian traders were pushing westward and southward from Hudson Bay and Lake Winnipeg. The French and Spanish at the village of St. Louis reacted to this pressure by expanding their trade up the river onto the lands of the northern plains Indians.

The 1804-06 journey of Meriwether Lewis and William Clark to the Pacific dramatized the change of ownership of Louisiana from Spain to the United States. These American explorers described with accuracy the tributaries of the upper Missouri, such as the Yellowstone, and brought the news that the western mountains were rich in furs, particularly beaver.

Two years after Lewis and Clark completed their journey, John Jacob Astor, a sober German immigrant who had already acquired a small fortune in the fur trade and in trade with China, wrote New York State's most powerful politician, De Witt Clinton, then mayor of New York City. From his personal knowledge of the fur trade and from studying the operations of the British companies in Canada, Astor had developed some ideas "for carring on the furr trade in the united states in a manner even more extensive than it is Done by the comaneys in canada." He admitted his plan would require four or five years in order to get control of "the whole of the furr trade & to extend it to the weastern ocean." His transportation routes would be from both New York and New Orleans, "up the Missiccppie and to have a range of Posts or trading houses on the rout made by Captn Lewis to the Sea."[1]

Astor pursued his dream and, in the spring of 1808, the American Fur Company came into existence. The organizational growth of the company during the next 26 years would be a major study in itself, yet it is necessary to note certain stages, subsidiary companies, and personalities along the way. One such name is that of Ramsay Crooks.

Born in Scotland, Crooks had come to Canada while still a teenager. After working briefly for the fur traders based in Montreal, he appeared in St. Louis where he joined Astor's Pacific Fur Company when this subsidiary was formed in 1811. Crooks climbed rapidly and, by 1817, was a member of the exclusive top management of the American Fur Company.[2]

Although the Pacific Fur Company lost out to British traders on the Pacific Coast during the War of 1812, Astor solidified his position at the same time in the Great Lakes area through another subsidiary, the South West Company (i.e., southwest of Montreal).[3] In the spring of 1821, Astor acknowledged Crooks's contributions to this period of the firm's growth by increasing Ramsay's share in the company to one-fifth of the whole.[4] The two men now felt ready to take on the opposition for control of the Missouri River and the Rocky Mountain trade.

Later that year, Crooks sent an agent to St. Louis to negotiate with fur companies based there. At first, this agent met with stubborn resistance as the pride of St. Louis turned a deaf ear to the upstarts from the East. But, by 1823, the American Fur Company succeeded in establishing its presence in St. Louis when Stone, Bostwick, and Company agreed to serve as its agent.[5]

At this time the Company underwent still another reorganization. The Great Lakes area was renamed the Northern Department; while the hoped-for but as yet unrealized developments out of St. Louis were named the Western Department. Ramsay Crooks took over the management of both departments.[6]

Astor, though spending an increasing amount of time in Europe now, continued to fret about the slowness of the Western Department's expansion, especially up the Missouri River. Two opposition companies, Bernard Pratte and Company and the Columbia Fur Company, were particularly successful in keeping Astor's men restricted pretty much to the role of buyers at St. Louis.[7]

At this time, four St. Louis men of French descent composed the firm of Bernard Pratte and Company: Pratte himself, Pierre Chouteau, Jr., John P. Cabanne, and Bartholomew Berthold, all members of important families. Mrs. Pratte and Pierre Chouteau, Jr., were first cousins. These two cousins demonstrated both the feudalistic organization of French society in St. Louis and the problem that Astor faced in trying to break into this society.[8] So spirited was the competition offered by Pratte's company that, in 1827, Astor gave up trying to break it and came to terms with it. A contract was arranged finally by which Bernard Pratte and Company assumed control of the Western Department.[9] Further cementing the ties between the two companies was Ramsay Crooks's marriage two years earlier to Bernard Pratte's daughter, Emilie.[10]

Crooks next turned his attention to the Columbia Fur Company. This dynamic, cocky organization was composed mostly of ex-employees of Canada's North West Company who had migrated to St. Louis after that company merged with the Hudson's Bay Company in the early 1820s. To overcome the law restricting foreigners in the fur trade, an American named Tilton became the head of the company. But he was just a figurehead; the real leader was Kenneth McKenzie.[11]

Like Crooks, McKenzie had been born in Scotland. He migrated to Canada before he was 20 and became a clerk in the North West Company. After he arrived in St. Louis in 1822, he applied for American citizenship, which he eventually acquired. Beyond anyone's doubt he was the ablest member of the Columbia Fur Company. McKenzie was a ruthless, proud man; his ambitions were matched by his abilities to realize them.[12]

Crooks began his courtship of the Columbia Fur Company as early as the summer of 1826. McKenzie reacted by setting up conditions that the American Fur Company could not accept. Undiscouraged, Crooks wrote McKenzie, "I am still disposed to arrange for the future provided you are inclined to be moderate in your expectations." Crooks saw the futility of trying to reach agreement by writing letters and proposed that the two Scotsmen meet at Fort Snelling "next April or perhaps even earlier."[13]

In May 1827, Crooks reported to Astor, then in New York, that he had met with McKenzie twice (though not at Fort Snelling) and "I must say he was as frank as a prudent man ought to be." Moreover, "to secure even Mr. McKenzie would be very desirable for he is certainly the soul of his concern." Astor learned in this letter that McKenzie would not come over to the American Fur Company unless some of his associates came with him.[14] This demand was easily accommodated, for McKenzie wished to include only the more competent of his associates.

Negotiations continued in St. Louis throughout June. Crooks realized he was up against a hard bargainer; on July 6, however, he informed Astor "that after an almost endless negociation [sic] I have at last succeeded in agreeing on preliminaries with the Columbia Fur Company to give up their trade entirely and take a share with us in that of the Upper Missouri."[15]

The structure of the American Fur Company was now virtually complete; only the Rocky Mountain trade still lay outside its grasp. Astor and Crooks oversaw the whole operation, with Crooks actively concerned with the management of both the Northern and Western Departments. The Northern Department held a near monopoly in its area of operations, while the Western Department, now with both Chouteau and McKenzie in its folds, was ready to take control of the upper Missouri and to challenge any and all who dared to compete. McKenzie was placed in charge of the upper river, and his organization's name was changed from Columbia Fur Company to Upper Missouri Outfit, abbreviated in correspondence and seals to UMO. Never subservient—indeed as independent as before—the Upper Missouri Outfit worked with Bernard Pratte and Company and the American Fur Company in the manner of an associate rather than as a subordinate. But as far as the general public and the opposition traders were concerned, the whole organization was known as the American Fur Company.[16]

The agreement was not the end of Crooks's work in St. Louis that summer. Pierre Chouteau, Jr.'s, health was very poor for the moment, and he was not up to supervising the preparation of outfits for the upper Missouri. Besides that, Crooks concluded, Pierre needed a little more training in the methods employed by the American Fur Company. Thus Crooks remained in the humid city overseeing the departure of the outfits for the newly-acquired empire.[17]

Crooks was soon to learn that he did not have to worry about Chouteau's stamina. Known in his family as Cadet (i.e., Junior), Pierre was soon to prove himself as the most dynamic leader in the St. Louis fur industry. Born in the city in 1789, he had become a clerk for his father, Pierre, Sr., when 15 years old. He had traveled up the Missouri as early as 1809 and, as the years passed, added to his knowledge and experience of handling men and furs. In the

Kenneth McKenzie. *Courtesy Missouri Historical Society, St. Louis.*

next few years, his increasing stature would show itself in the name changes of his company, first to Pratte, Chouteau & Company; then, with Pratte's retirement in 1838, to Pierre Chouteau, Jr., & Company.

Chouteau, described by DeVoto as a financier with an "empire-building mind, hard, brilliant, daring, speculative, and ruthless," recovered his strength and assumed his responsibilities. Soon he would be advising his associates, **"erasez toute opposition**," and employing every stratagem necessary to that end.[18]

The inventories of the former posts of the Columbia Fur Company were completed by 1828. Crooks wrote to Chouteau, "I am rejoiced to find our new ally Mr. McKenzie was so reasonable in adjusting to matters connected with the Inventories."[19] By the fall of 1828, McKenzie was ready to build the citadel from which he would rule the upper Missouri. He would be called King by both enemy and friend; the seat of his kingdom would be called Fort Union.

Notes

1. John Jacob Astor, January 1808, to DeWitt Clinton, Astor Papers, vol. 44, Baker Library, Harvard University.

2. Hiram Martin Chittenden, **The American Fur Trade of the Far West**, 2 vols. (New York: Press of the Pioneers, 1935), 1:380-81.

3. Kenneth Wiggins Porter, **John Jacob Astor, Business Man**, 2 vols. (New York: Russell & Russell, 1966), 2:750. LeRoy R. Hafen, **The Mountain Men and the Fur Trade of the Far West**, 10 vols. (Glendale: The Arthur H. Clark Co., 1965-72), 1:105. Astor joined the Michilimackinac Company, a subsidiary of the North West Company (Canadian), to form the South West Company, 1811. In 1816, a law was enacted excluding foreigners from control of the fur trade in the United States. This law encouraged the Canadian members of the company to sell out to Astor in 1817.

4. John Jacob Astor, March 27, 1821, to Ramsay Crooks, John Jacob Astor Papers, New York Public Library.

5. Paul Chrisler Phillips, **The Fur Trade**, 2 vols. (Norman: University of Oklahoma Press, 1961), 2:402.

6. **Ibid** 2:402. Porter, 2:750. Hafen, 1:105.

7. Phillips, 2:404-05.

8. The original Chouteau in St. Louis was Rene Auguste, grandfather of Pierre, Jr. Rene helped Lacléde Liquest found the city. Biographical details of the Chouteau family may be found in Chittenden, **American Fur Trade**, 1:113n, and William Hyde and Howard L. Conard, eds., **Encyclopedia of the History of St. Louis**, (New York, 1899).

9. Chittenden, **American Fur Trade**, 1:331. Phillips, 2:405-06.

10. Chittenden, **American Fur Trade**, 1:380-81. Although Crooks became Pratte's son-in-law, this did not lessen a dislike for Pratte that Astor had developed.

11. At this time, McKenzie signed his name in this manner. Later in life, he changed it to Mackenzie. See Annie Heloise Abel, **Chardon's Journal at Fort Clark, 1834-1839** (Pierre: State of South Dakota, 1932), p. 273, note 267.

12. Phillips, 2:407-09. Other members of the Columbia Fur Company were William Laidlaw, James Kipp, Joseph Renville, Honoré Picotte, and Daniel Lamont.

13. Ramsay Crooks, August 30, 1826, to Kenneth McKenzie, Ramsay Crooks Papers, Detroit Public Library.

14. Ramsay Crooks, May 24, 1827, to John J. Astor, **Ibid**.

15. Crooks, July 6, 1827, to Astor, **Ibid**

16. The organization and the relationships between the posts is fully discussed in Phillips, 2:417-19, and Chittenden, **American Fur Trade**, 1:327-28.

17. Crooks, August 10, 1827, to Astor, Crooks Papers, Detroit Public Library.

18. Hariette Johnson Westbrook, "The Chouteaus and Their Commercial Enterprises," **Chronicles of Oklahoma** 11 (1933):790-95. Hyde and Conard, **Encyclopedia**, 1:363-65. Chittenden, **American Fur Trade**, 1:366-67. Bernard DeVoto, **Across the Wide Missouri** (Boston: Houghton Mifflin, 1947), p. 69.

19. Crooks, September 14, 1828, to Chouteau, Envelope for August-December 1865, Chouteau Collections, 1828-1869, Missouri Historical Society, hereinafter cited as Chouteau Coll., MoHS. See also Chittenden, **American Fur Trade**, 1:328, who gives the last inventory date as on December 5, 1827.

CHAPTER 2

A Fort is Needed

Between the time Captain Meriwether Lewis had camped nearby in the spring of 1805 and the arrival of Kenneth McKenzie in the area, the junction of the Missouri and the Yellowstone had witnessed the fires of many whites. In the fall of 1822, Andrew Henry and William H. Ashley, considered to be the innovators of the annual rendezvous system in the Rockies, built a small post at the meeting point of the two streams. However, Henry found this location to be farther from the beaver country than he liked, and he soon moved his establishment up the Yellowstone.[1]

Three years later, 1825, Brigadier General Henry Atkinson led a considerable number of troops to the junction, which a diarist described as "the most beautiful spot we have seen on the river." The soldiers found the ruins of Henry's fort, and somewhere near it set up a temporary camp they called Barbour. A portion of the troops remained here while the rest escorted the Indian agent, Benjamin O'Fallon, up the Missouri to meet with the less-than-friendly Blackfeet. The entire command soon descended the river again for the benefits of civilization.[2]

About this same time, James Kipp, an associate of Kenneth McKenzie in the Columbia Fur Company, founded a post at the

9

junction of the Missouri and White Earth rivers, among the Assiniboins. While this post was some distance below the mouth of the Yellowstone, it was closer than any other and provided Kipp, McKenzie, and the others a location from which to become better acquainted with the trade potential of the upper country.[3]

McKenzie, now in charge of the Upper Missouri Outfit, decided to build a post near the mouth of the Yellowstone. Here he could trade with the Assiniboins, who wandered the prairies toward the north; with the Crows, located up the Yellowstone; and perhaps with the Blackfeet, farther up the Missouri. From here also expeditions could be organized for the Rocky Mountains (he had wanted to get involved more directly with the mountain trade, but Pierre Chouteau, Jr., had persuaded him that the upper Missouri would be more profitable). If the post was efficient enough, it could also attract the trade of the free, or unassociated, trappers throughout the country.

Only one or two historians have, over the years, offered documented evidence as to the date McKenzie started his new fort. One such was Hiram Chittenden, who quoted from a letter, now lost, that McKenzie had established a fort near the mouth of the Yellowstone at least as early as December 1828, and that this post was called Fort Floyd.[4]

Chittenden also quoted, in French, from a letter written by Pierre Chouteau, Jr., to William Astor, John Jacob's son. The present whereabouts of this letter, dated April 19, 1830, is also unknown. The translation reads:

> On my arrival here (St. Louis) on the 16th [April, 1830], I found a letter from Mr. McKenzie of 28 December, 1829, and ones dated 2 and 20 January [1830], 200 miles above the Yellow Stone. The mountain hunters were not as successful in the fall hunt as he had hoped, but he hopes for more success in the spring. It is his opinion that there will be more robes this year than is the usual case; that is to say in the three upper posts, at the Mandans, at the mouth of the Yellow Stone, and Fort Union 200 miles above, and he says that the upper country is very rich in beaver and robes.[5]

This is the earliest known reference to a Fort Union, even though this Fort Union was or was to be 200 miles above the junction. The letter is not at all clear as to whether this Fort Union was built or was still in the planning stage. As far as it may be otherwise determined, the Upper Missouri Outfit did not have any forts that far up the river at that time. The letter does imply, of course, that McKenzie was 200 miles up the Missouri beyond the junction for a good part of January 1830.

Considering both sources, one must assume there was a Fort Floyd. But it is not shown that this Fort Floyd was at the same location as Fort Union is known to have been, nor is it shown that the upriver Fort Union mentioned by Chouteau was ever built.

Two letters by William Laidlaw, another ex-Columbia man, now at Fort Tecumseh, tell us that McKenzie was on the upper Missouri in 1829. One of them, dated August 13, said that "McKenzie left here about 25 days ago for the Upper Country   he was able to take with him a tolerable aportment of goods." Two months later, on October 26, Laidlaw wrote, "The last news from McKensie [sic] he was at white earth river waiting for the summer boat, after her arrival he was to proceed up to the mouth of Yellow Stone river and winter there."[6]

Did McKenzie return to the Fort Floyd he mentioned the previous December? If so, did this fort evolve into Fort Union? The available evidence answers with a resounding silence. Prince Maximilian, a visitor to Fort Union in 1833, learned that "the erection of Fort Union was commenced in the autumn of 1829, by Mr. McKenzie."[7] Since the prince undoubtedly got this information directly from his good friend, McKenzie, it should not be ignored. Edwin T. Denig, who knew the fort well, made a similar statement in 1843, "The fort itself was begun in the fall of 1829, under the superintendence of Kenneth McKenzie."[8]

Despite Chittenden's belief that Fort Union grew out of Fort Floyd and thus its founding date was 1828, this report will assume that Fort Union was founded in the fall of 1829, when McKenzie went up to the junction of the two rivers from Fort Tecumseh. And it will assume that Fort Union did not evolve out of Fort Floyd, a post of some nature that is found in the documents by name but once.

The earliest mention of the name Union, as applied to the known historic site, was in a letter that Kenneth McKenzie sent to the "Gentleman in charge of Fort Tecumseh," which he dated Fort Union, May 5, 1830, less than three weeks after Chouteau applied the name to a site 200 miles upstream.[9] In this letter McKenzie asked that various supplies be sent up. From the list, one may determine that both trade (beaver traps, shirts) and construction (pit-saw files) were actively under way. He also wanted sent up his "gray mare & her colt and John Dougherty's little mare." McKenzie was planning to stay.

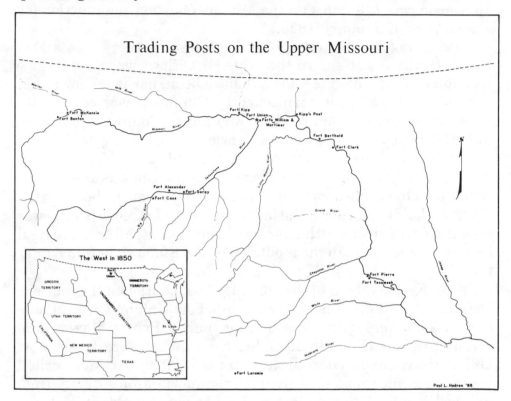

He had reason to believe that the fort was well located. One would have looked up and down the Missouri vainly for a better location in this general area. Rather than locate the post right at the junction, where the land was level but low, McKenzie picked a high spot on the north bank of the Missouri about five miles by water above the junction.[10] There was a considerable growth of trees on points immediately above and below this site, trees which would supply both building timbers and firewood. The site was at least 20 feet above the river, high enough to be safe from the annual floods. The ground here was a level prairie that stretched away to the north for a mile or so, thus providing ample space for the Indian camps at trading time. Farther off to the northeast was a sizeable coulee that led down from the high prairies beyond the skyline; this coulee would provide an avenue of approach to the fort for the Assiniboins. And, perhaps most important, the river ran close to this bank, thus allowing boats to tie up near the fort and reducing the portage of cargo to but a few feet.[11]

12

This was the country of the big sky, the immense herds of buffalo, the high plains, and the Indians of the tipi. But it was not entirely a paradise. Nearly always, strong winds tore across the prairies, mosquitoes plagued man and beast in the spring and summer, and the winters were long and bitterly cold. One employee wrote that the post was "exposed to every wind that blows from any point of the compass, is said to be the coldest place of all the posts belonging to this company—even as cold as those situated on Hudson Bay."[12] The fort would have to be firmly built.

Notes

1. Phillips, 2:396-97.

2. Russell Reid and Clell G. Gannon, eds. "Journal of the Atkinson-O'Fallon Expedition," **North Dakota Historical Quarterly** 4 (1929):41 and 41n.

3. James Kipp was one of the associates who remained with McKenzie in the Upper Missouri Outfit. He was born in Montreal, P. Q. His first experience in the fur trade was in the Red River area. By 1818, he was on the Missouri where he had a long career, retiring in 1865. Kipp was well liked by the various Indians, and he developed the reputation of fort builder. See Ray H. Mattison, "James Kipp," in Hafen, 1:201-05; and Abel, p.225, n.80.

4. Chittenden, **American Fur Trade,** 2:933, quoting from a letter written by McKenzie at Fort Tecumseh, March 15, 1829: "Your favor of the 5th of December [1828] reached me on the 25th ult., the date of my arrival from Fort Floyd near the Yellowstone."

5. **Ibid,** 2:933. The translation is by the writer.

6. William Laidlaw, Fort Tecumseh, August 13 and October 26, 1829, to Pierre Chouteau, Jr., Folder 1829—August and September, Chouteau Coll. MoHS. Chittenden described William Laidlaw as a severe man with a tyrannical temper, but who was, next to McKenzie, the best trader in the old Columbia Fur Company. See Chittenden, **American Fur Trade,** 1:385-86.

7. Reuben Gold Thwaites, ed., **Maximilian's Travels in the Interior of North America, 1832-1834,** in Early Western Travels, 1748-1846, vol.22 (Cleveland: The Arthur H. Clark Co., 1906), p.376.

8. Maria R. Audubon, **Audubon and His Journals,** 2 vols. (New York: Dover Publication, 1960), 2:181.

9. McKenzie, Fort Union, May 5, 1830, to "Gentleman in charge of Fort Tecumseh," Folder January-May, 1830, Chouteau Coll., MoHS. The first time the name "Fort Union" has been found in the account books of the American Fur Company was under the date of August 7, 1830, in an account for the UMO. See Account Book "R," April 1829-November 1832, p.211, Upper Missouri Outfit, 1830, American Fur Company, MoHS.

10. Five miles is an arbitrary distance. Most visitors in the early days gave a figure in that vicinity. Today, the distance is only about three miles. This variation was and is caused by the meanders of both streams within their valleys.

11. The Missouri wandered freely from one side of the "bottoms" to the other. It apparently was fairly stable in the vicinity of Fort Union, however. The records mention only one time when boats had to tie up some distance from the fort. Today, the river is about 400 yards to the south.

12. Rudolph Friederich Kurz, **Journal of Rudolph Friederich Kurz,** trans. Myrtis Jarrell, ed. J. N. B. Hewitt, Smithsonian Institution, Bureau of American Ethnology Bulletin 115 (Washington: U.S. Government Printing Office, 1937), p.168.

CHAPTER 3

Palisades and Princes

The letter books of the period do not describe the beginning of construction of Fort Union. Chittenden, noting James Kipp's experience at fort building, has suggested that most likely he was the supervisor of the work. Another writer has stated that **métis** laborers did the actual work.[1] While there may have been some métis employed at the fort, it is more probable that the skilled workmen (carpenters, masons) came from St. Louis and that the large majority of the laborers were French Canadian **engagés,** from Quebec. The American Fur Company regularly had a recruiter in Quebec, and a new batch of forty-three **mangeurs du lard** had arrived at Fort Tecumseh in August 1829.[2]

The first task involved the cutting and hewing of suitable timber and hauling it to the site. A stout palisade of vertical logs soon enclosed a quadrangle 220 by 240 feet. The long axis of the fort ran almost due north and south; while the shorter sides paralleled the river. The apartments of the employees occupied a long building on the western side of the interior. A similar building containing the storerooms and the retail store stood opposite, on the east side. At the north end stood the bourgeois's house and, behind it, a kitchen. In the western half of the north end was a large but simple gate that led out on to the prairie. On the front, or southern end, were the main gate, a reception room for Indians, and shops for various tradesmen such as the blacksmith and the tinner. Other, smaller structures stood here and there around the perimeter. At the northeast and southwest corners stood imposing, two-story, stone bastions. In the center of the court a tall flagstaff reached for the sky.

The first international visitor to Fort Union arrived in May 1830, when Prince Paul, or Duke Paul Wilhelm of Württemberg, a southern German state, arrived on his second trip to the United States. Although a major general in the army of Frederick II of Prussia and related to most of the reigning monarchs of Europe, Prince Paul was interested in neither the military nor court life. Instead, he dedicated himself to exploring the far corners of the world; at that time, Fort Union qualified as a far corner. His biographer states that Prince Paul was a "fine sketch artist," but no results of his pen have been found. His work was destroyed during the air raids on Germany in World War II.[3]

While no written account by Prince Paul seems to have survived, there is a record of his purchases at Fort Union.[4] They show him to have been rather an easy spender. Between May 17 and August 2, he ran up a bill of $714.15. This sum can be broken down to show expenditures in buying trade goods, necessary supplies such as powder and ball, specimens of Indian handicraft, liquor, and pay for servants supplied by the company.[5] Although he seems to have paid his bill in full at Fort Union, Prince Paul returned to Germany owing money to Pratte, Chouteau, and Co. Later, in 1833, John Jacob Astor wrote his son from Europe that Prince Paul "has neither money nor credit, but he hopes to get the amount of your [Chouteau's] claim in the course of a few months."[6]

Another prince who visited Fort Union in 1830 was Tchatka, an Assiniboin. For most of the time that Fort Union was in existence, there was little danger of an attack by the Assiniboins, or anyone else. However, in this year, Tchatka, or le Gaucher, offered a very real threat. Having lost face among his followers when he suffered a defeat at the hands of the Blackfeet, le Gaucher attempted to regain his lost prestige by offering his 200 followers a scheme whereby to capture the fort. Arriving at the post, he persuaded McKenzie to believe that his men were on their way to attack Minnitarees and he asked for powder.

Despite the stout palisades, it was often the custom at Fort Union to allow trusted Indians to sleep inside the fort; on this occasion,

McKenzie gave such permission. At bedtime, le Gaucher's men retired to the various rooms to which they had been assigned. According to the plan, they were to await a signal from le Gaucher, at which time they would attack their white roommates.

One of the white employees had an Assiniboin wife whose brother, one of the attackers, warned her of the plan. She, in turn, passed the warning on. McKenzie acted as if he knew nothing. During the night, he summoned the eighty-odd employees then at the fort to come to the main house, a few at a time. He armed his men and had them occupy the stone bastions and other strategic points. When his men were ready, McKenzie had le Gaucher brought to his room. He informed the chief of his awareness of the attack and gave him the opportunity to leave peacefully before the whites opened fire. The Assiniboins left.[7]

McKenzie traveled down the river in the summer of 1830. When he returned to Fort Union, he found there a trapper by the name of Berger. This old-timer had learned the Blackfoot language when working for the British. Until now, nearly every effort by Americans to trade with the Blackfeet or to hunt in their territory, which lay above Fort Union, had ended in an attack by the Indians. McKenzie persuaded Berger to visit the upper tributaries and to talk the Blackfeet into sending a delegation to Fort Union. Berger was successful in this effort in 1831, and the Blackfeet agreed to let McKenzie send James Kipp up to trade. This resulted in the eventual establishment of Fort McKenzie near the mouth of Marias River. McKenzie's success with the Blackfeet, where other American traders had failed, increased his stature as king of the upper Missouri.

Later, he turned his attention to the Crows on the Yellowstone and, in 1832, established Fort Cass at the mouth of the Big Horn River. This made Fort Union the pivot point for the upper reaches of both rivers; its storerooms supplied the trade goods and stored the furs and robes.[8]

A few months before the establishment of Fort Cass, McKenzie almost lost Fort Union to fire. In the middle of the night, February 3, 1832, shouts of "Fire!" woke him up. He ran from his house to find blazing "the range of buildings forming the west quadrangle of the fort (120 ft. by 24 ft.) and occupied by the clerks, interpreters, mechanics, and engagees, with their families, of squalling children not a few."

In describing the origins and results of the fire, McKenzie made mention of some structural details. The fire began in Francis Chardon's room, "originating beneath the floor, and there being . . . a free communication under the whole range, and much rubbish . . . it was almost simultaneous in every department." Among the items destroyed were trunks of clothing, a year's collection of buffalo tongues, rifles, pistols, and rare white beaver skins. McKenzie described both a loft and a cellar. The loft contained nearly 1,000 planks, stored there to season and which had taken two men six months to saw. The cellar was full of small kegs. Today, there is a depression in the ground about where the northwest room of this "range" should be.

The meat house was also threatened by the fire, but it survived. Also of great worry to McKenzie was a supply of gunpowder kept in the storeroom on the east side. By four a.m., however, the fire was under control. Besides the line of quarters, most of the west wall also burned. Quarters were found for the homeless, and repairs of the wall began immediately. The men cut 170 trees on the next day and five days later had replaced all the burnt pickets. McKenzie wrote that it would be "months before the buildings can be reinstated. In our wooden houses I fear we are all too little cautious."[9] By early summer, most of the fire scars had disappeared and it was time for the boats from St. Louis.

Until 1832, the principal craft on the upper Missouri for hauling supplies upstream was the keelboat. A crew of twenty to forty men pulled this craft against the current by means of a line, or cordelle. Occasionally the wind would be strong enough to use sails; from time to time conditions of the water or the banks would force the crew to pole or to row. All the time, getting a cargo the 2,000 miles from St. Louis to Fort Union was desperately hard work.[10]

McKenzie believed that the transportation problem could be greatly reduced by employing a properly designed steamboat on the Missouri. Snags, boiler explosions, and mechanical breakdowns would be dangers, but danger awaited all kinds of craft when the river was in a rage. McKenzie finally persuaded Pierre Chouteau, Jr., to invest in the building of a shallow-draft steamboat. In 1831, the **Yellow Stone** puffed as far as Fort Tecumseh, about two-thirds of the way to Fort Union.

Writing from Paris in the summer of 1832, John Jacob Astor asked, "How did the Yellow Stone behave, and what said the Indians about her?" He soon got the answer. McKenzie's idea was a success; the **Yellow Stone** reached Fort Union about the middle of June.[11]

Aboard was Pierre Chouteau, Jr., himself, who had had a fine time coming up, including a stopover to christen the rebuilt fort at Tecumseh as Fort Pierre. John F. Sanford, a sub-Indian agent

Steamboat *Yellow Stone* at St. Louis. George Catlin painted this scene, probably in 1832, when he visited Fort Union aboard this vessel, the first steamboat to reach the junction of the Missouri and Yellowstone rivers. *Courtesy National Museum of American Art, Smithsonian Institution.*

who married Pierre's daughter, Emilie, was also a passenger.[12] But the passenger destined to become more widely known than they was George Catlin, America's first artist on the upper Missouri. Scorned by artists who later visited Fort Union, Catlin has survived the passing decades; and his portraits of far-western Indians are today recognized as a substantial contribution to art and to ethnology.[13]

However, Catlin's two sketches of Fort Union leave much to be desired by the historian. One of these is a mere scribble, possibly done aboard the steamboat approaching the post.[14] The other is a finished painting that Catlin displayed in his European exhibits. This is not a great drawing of the distant fort either, although it does catch the appearance of the country. On the other hand, the drawing is not as bad as its critics have maintained.[15]

In the end, Catlin earned a reputation of hastiness and awkwardness. John C. Ewers points out, however, that during the eighty-six days Catlin spent on the Missouri, he produced more than 135 pictures, a very large output for so short a time.[16]

Of greater interest than his paintings are Catlin's comments on Fort Union. The post struck him as "a very substantial Fort . . . with bastions armed with ordnance, and our approach to it under the continued roar of cannon for half an hour, and the shrill yells of the half-affrighted savages who lined the shores, presented a scene of the most thrilling appearance." Catlin noted that Union was "the largest and best-built establishment of the kind on the river, being the great or principal head-quarters and depot of the Fur Company's business in this region."

During the next few days, he learned other details of the post "which contains some eight or ten log-houses and stores, and has generally forty or fifty men." Among the buildings already in use was the all-important and "spacious" ice house, used for preserving meat and cooling drinks. He noted, too, that McKenzie had a scow for crossing to the south bank, a boat large enough to ferry one-horse carts. Catlin did not say where he slept, but he reported using one of the bastions as a painting room, "My easel stands before me, and the cool breech of a twelve-pounder makes me a comfortable seat, whilst her muzzle is looking out at one of the port-holes."

Indians were allowed into the fort to watch Catlin paint. He observed that when they entered they had to place their weapons in the "arsenal." He was the only one to use this term; it is difficult to determine what room was used for this purpose.

Catlin was as much impressed with McKenzie as he was with the post. He described the king as "a kind-hearted and high-minded Scotsman," who "lives in good and comfortable style." McKenzie's table "groans under the luxuries of the country; with buffalo meat and tongues, with beavers' tails and marrow-fat; but," strangely enough, "_sans_ coffee, _sans_ bread and butter. Good cheer and good living we get at it however, and good wine also, for a bottle of Madeira and one of excellent Port are set in a pail of ice every day, and exhausted at dinner."

The artist also met James Archdale Hamilton, another of the unusual characters at Fort Union. Hamilton was an Englishman of exceptionally good education. His associates believed him to be a nobleman whose real name was Archibald Palmer. Considered to be a good host, but an eccentric man, Hamilton hated Indians, a rather odd attitude considering his environment. The French Canadian employees were said to hold him in awe because he took a bath and put on a clean shirt every day.[17] Catlin described Hamilton as a gentleman who was "a complete store-house of ancient and modern literature and art."

Besides the Assiniboins, Catlin had the opportunity to study both Blackfeet and Crees when a band of each came in at the same time. To keep them from fighting, McKenzie had them camp on opposite sides of the fort, out on the prairie, and he disarmed them for the duration of their stay. That he could enforce such acts was an acknowledgment of his great power. According to Catlin, there was no trouble until the Crees broke camp. At the last minute, one of them poked "the muzzle of his gun through the piquets [sic] and fatally wounded a Blackfoot inside the fort."[18]

The Indians would call the steamboats the "Fire Boats that walked on the waters;" and the successful trip of the **Yellow Stone** introduced the beginning of a new period of travel on the upper Missouri. Fort Union was already on its way to being the most handsome of posts; now, with the ease of transportation, McKenzie and his successors would turn it into an establishment almost luxurious in nature. News of the boat's success was carried by newspapers in both America and Europe. Astor wrote from France, "your voyage in the yellow stone attracted much attention in Europe & has been notiesed in all the Papers here." Crooks wrote Chouteau, "I congratulate you most cordially on your perseverance and ultimate success in reaching the Yellow Stone **by steam** and the future Historian of Missouri will preserve for you the honorable and enviable distinction of having accomplished an object of immense importance."[19]

For the moment, the American Fur Company had complete control over the upper Missouri and its tributaries. But it did not yet control the Rocky Mountain trade; now, from that region, came the threat of opposition. Robert Campbell had left Northern Ireland in 1824 and had migrated to St. Louis because of poor health. Before long, he entered the fur trade wherein he met up with William Sublette, one of several brothers who collectively were known throughout the length and breadth of the far west. At the end of 1832, the two formed a partnership and planned to challenge the American Fur Company by erecting a competing fort next to every company post along the Missouri.

In the summer of 1833, Campbell led a group of traders overland to the mouth of the Yellowstone where he met Sublette, who had come up the Missouri by steamboat with supplies and trade goods. Near the junction, on the same side of the river as Fort Union and about two and one-half miles below as the crow flies, the partners began building the wooden establishment, Fort William, named for Sublette.[20]

One of their employees, Charles Larpenteur, described the fort as being 150 by 130 feet, located 200 yards from the Missouri, precisely where Fort Buford's sawmill would stand in the 1870s. The fifteen-foot stockade was made of cottonwood, with an additional three feet planted in the ground. The bourgeois's house was a cabin of two rooms separated by a breezeway. In addition, there were two rooms for men's quarters, a combination store and warehouse, ice and meat houses, various shops, "and two splendid bastions." The entire complex was finished by Christmas, an indication of its inferiority to Fort Union, which took over four years to complete.[21]

Sublette, sick ever since he arrived, went back to St. Louis after three weeks. His departure would mean trouble for Kenneth McKenzie, as will be later noted. Campbell, supplied with a large quantity of illicit liquor, set out to capture the Indian trade from McKenzie.[22] McKenzie, also well supplied with alcohol, was determined to destroy Fort William economically. By the end of the year, Campbell would learn just how ruthless McKenzie could be.

The irritations began in the fall. When Campbell made an offer to sell out, McKenzie turned him down. He would rather force Campbell out than buy him out. A few days later, Campbell learned that two men had found a packet of beaver that he had lost the past summer and had sold the beaver to McKenzie. Campbell went up to Fort Union to argue that the furs were his, but without success. Next, he discovered that François Deschamps, an employee, was actually a spy for McKenzie. Worst of all, "McKenzie gives as much wisky as the Indians can drink for nothing. Barrel after Barrel he sends all around amongst the Indians and those will not trade otherwise."[23]

On New Year's Eve, Campbell was wholly discouraged, "I can safely say as unhappy a time as this I have never before passed during my life. What is worst our prospects are not good for McKenzie has hired our interpreters and bribed them whilst they were here to betray us."[24]

McKenzie was almost enjoying his destruction of the opposition. In January 1834, he wrote, "although on their first start here, they made a great show and promise to the Indians and although among the men nothing was talked about but the new company, they live now at the sign of 'The case is altered.' Their interpreters have . . . left them and are now working hard for me." He concluded, "the new company is in bad odor and must sink."[25]

Then, in April 1834, just when McKenzie was sure of driving out Sublette and Campbell, Chouteau wrote him that he had bought out the opposition.[26] McKenzie was disappointed and not at all convinced that it had been necessary to have spent the money. His method would have been cheaper.

Before leaving Campbell and his fort, a further look at his journal is necessary. Several times in 1833 he was a guest at Fort Union, and his diary entries add to our information. In September he went up to visit Hamilton who had been ill. Being the gentleman, Hamilton showed Campbell "the buildings even to the Ice House and Stables and every convenience of the fort. The Ice House serves for Lumber having a door in the floor and a descent by rope ladder to the Ice."[27]

On December 15, Campbell made an entry in his journal of a disaster at Fort Union: "Last night two sides of McKenzies new fort was leveled with the ground" because of a strong wind. "He had built a stone and lime foundation and raised his pickets thereon but it appears something more substantial is required in this country to brave the winds."[28] Fort Union's carpenters solved this problem when they rebuilt the walls. Denig described the new construction: "This space is enclosed by pickets . . . twenty feet high, made of hewn cottonwood, and founded upon stone. The pickets are fitted into an open framework in the inside, of sufficient strength to counterbalance their weight, and sustained by braces in the form of an X, which reaches in the inside from the pickets to the frame, so as to make the whole completely solid and secure, from either storm or attack."[29] These braces may be seen in at least two of the sketches made of Fort Union's interior.

Campbell was also a visitor to Fort Union on the occasion of a dinner for Prince Maximilian of Wied, the second German prince to visit Fort Union. On October 2, Campbell wrote, "I received a note from Mr. Hamilton inviting me to dine and to be made acquaint[ed] with the Baron Bransburgh [Braunsberg, which Maximilian liked to call himself] or Prince of Newyd [Neuwied]." Campbell went up "and passed a pleasant evening in this society."[30]

The prince had arrived at Fort Union with McKenzie on June 24. Travelling with him were a Swiss artist, Karl Bodmer, and a secretary, Mr. Drydopple. After a few weeks at Union, the party traveled up to Fort McKenzie. When the prince returned to Fort Union that fall, he learned that McKenzie was again temporarily down the river. The prince remained for a few weeks as a guest

Karl Bodmer's depiction of the *Yellow Stone* aground on a sandbar while ascending the Missouri in 1833. The crew is rafting the cargo to shore to lighten the vessel.
Courtesy The InterNorth Art Foundation/Joslyn Art Museum, Omaha.

of Hamilton then went down to spend the winter at Fort Clark. Alexander Culbertson met Maximilian and thought he looked like anything but a prince—unostentatious, toothless, wearing greasy trousers and a worn black coat. Maximilian had considerable experience as a Prussian soldier, having been made a prisoner-of-war at Jena, and, like Prince Paul, a major general. In 1813 he had been in the allied army that had occupied Paris.[31] Now he was an explorer-scientist and committed to a simple manner of living.

Maximilian's journal gives an intimate look at Fort Union, beginning with his first view of the post late in the evening of June 24, 1833: "Fort Union, on a verdant plain, with the handsome American flag, gilded by the last rays of evening, floating in an azure sky, while a herd of horses grazing animated the peaceful scene." As the steamer approached, the fort's cannon fired a welcome salute. Hamilton came forth to greet the visitors, while the employees, "Americans, Englishmen, Germans, Frenchmen,

Russians, Spaniards, and Italians, about 100 in number, with many Indians, and half-breed women and children" welcomed the season's steamboat.

In describing the fort, Maximilian said that the river was only fifty to sixty feet from the front of the fort. To him the pickets seemed to be fifteen or sixteen feet high, "squared, and placed close to each other, and surmounted by chevaux-de-frise," or a barrier of spikes. He noted the large, folding gate at the front entrance, on the river side. Facing the gate stood the bourgeois's house, "one story high, and has four handsome glass windows on each side of the door. The roof is spacious, and contains a large, light loft. This house is very commodious, and, like all the buildings of the inner quadrangle, constructed of poplar wood [cottonwood?], the staple wood for building in this neighborhood." This is the earliest statement that in the beginning the main house was only one story high, a height that Bodmer's painting seems to confirm.

Maximilian also noted that several half-breed hunters had erected their tipis around the flagpole and that "a cannon was also placed here, with its mouth towards the principal entrance." Besides its personnel, the fort contained "about fifty or sixty horses, some mules, and an inconsiderable number of cattle, swine, goats, fowls, and domestic animals." He wrote that the horses were taken out on the prairie during the day, under guard, but were brought back inside each night. This was not too happy a situation, for it kept the yard very dirty, especially when it was wet. McKenzie was concerned about this and was planning a separate enclosure for the horses.

During the next few weeks, Maximilian's busy pen made notes on the fort, Indians, and the fur trade. In summing up the trade at Fort Union, he observed that buffalo hides (40,000 to 50,000) surpassed the number of beaver (25,000) skins. Other skins collected included otter, weasel, marten, lynx, red fox, cross fox, silver fox, mink, muskrat, and deer. The personnel of the fort, by themselves, consumed from 600 to 800 buffalo annually. He mentioned that corn was bought from neighboring tribes. He did not say that McKenzie used this corn in his still, but that is another story.

He learned that vegetables did not thrive but that mosquitoes did. He listed the birds and animals he saw and attempted to give a census of the Assiniboins, deciding there were 28,000, of whom 7,000 were warriors, and that they lived in 3,000 tipis. A few "wret-

Karl Bodmer's drawing of an Assiniboin encampment at Fort Union in 1833. The tipi in the foreground belonged to Ayanyan or Jackson, who had visited President Andrew Jackson in Washington, D.C. *Courtesy The InterNorth Art Foundation/Joslyn Art Museum, Omaha.*

chedly poor" Indians were at the fort when the prince arrived. He wrote that "several apartments in the fort were assigned to these visitors, where they cooked and slept."

As for himself and his companions, they had "a comfortable lodging" in McKenzie's house, "and we lived here very pleasantly, in a plain style, suitable to the resources of so remote a place." The prince did better than Catlin in that he had coffee as well as wine every day, along with buffalo flesh and bread.

Very shortly after Maximilian arrived, a large number of Assiniboins came in, impressing the Europeans greatly:

> Towards the northwest, the whole prairie was covered with scattered Indians, whose numerous dogs drew the sledges with the baggage; a close body of warriors, about 250 or 300 in number, had formed themselves in the center, in the manner of two bodies of infantry, and advanced in quick time towards the fort. The Indian warriors marched in close ranks, three or four men deep, not keeping their file very regularly, yet in pretty good order,

and formed a considerable line. Before the center . . . three or four chiefs advanced, arm in arm, and from the ranks . . . loud musket-shots were heard. The whole troop of these warriors now commenced their original song . . . many abrupt, broken tones. . . . The loaded dogs, guided by

Karl Bodmer's painting of a proud young Assiniboin man at Fort Union, 1833. The Assiniboins were the principal tribe to come to Fort Union. *Courtesy The Inter-North Art Foundation/Joslyn Art Museum, Omaha.*

women and children, surrounded the nucleus of warriors.

They advanced to within about sixty paces, then halted at a fosse [a ditch, or small ravine] running from the Missouri past the fort, and waited, the chief standing in front, for our welcome.

Maximilian realized that he was witnessing an event, a way of life, that would disappear from the American scene as fast as man could destroy it. His vivid description fixes permanently the image of that way of life.

When Maximilian left, July 6, for Fort McKenzie among the Blackfeet, McKenzie had a fireworks display set off along the bank of the river, hoisted the American flag, and fired several guns. No prince, German or otherwise, could ever complain about the hospitality.

When he returned in the autumn, the prince found "the whole prairie naked, dry, and withered." Instead of hundreds of Assiniboins, there was but one tent, inhabited by a half-Blackfoot. The Missouri itself was "shallow, narrow, and full of sand banks." McKenzie had gone; there were only fifty persons at the fort under the control of Mr. Hamilton.

During the absence of the prince, several improvements had occurred at the fort. Referring to the fire of 1832, he noted that "a handsome solid powder magazine, of hewn stone, which was capable of containing 50,000 lbs. of powder, was completed." He noted too that a rail fence, which had to be renovated, was almost finished. Another fence, the one around McKenzie's house, "was damaged by a horse chewing on it even though it had been painted reddish brown."

Maximilian had gathered a large number of specimens and souvenirs by this time and, to his great pleasure, Hamilton gave him the "spacious loft" in the bourgeois's house where he could take everything out of the boxes and barrels to dry and air. Bodmer also was given "a good clear room" in which to paint. Out of his efforts came a number of superb paintings which were later reproduced and made famous. The most important to the purposes here was one of Fort Union from the north. It was the first detailed illustration known to have been done.

As their time for departure neared, the visitors went on a buffalo hunt. Among the post employees to accompany them was McKenzie's Black slave. Maximilian noted other persons he met at the fort, such as Robert Campbell, the bourgeois at Fort William,

Fort Union in 1833. Karl Bodmer made this first detailed drawing of Fort Union
Trading Post. Besides the two bastions, it shows a blockhouse over the main gate
(far side). The roofline of the bourgeois's house shows it as the one-and-one-half
story structure it first was. *Courtesy The InterNorth Art Foundation/Joslyn Art Museum, Omaha.*

who came up to Union for dinner with the prince. He recorded too
those cool fall evenings, when he visited Hamilton in his apart-
ment and sat by the fireplace enjoying good punch and good
conversation.

When Maximilian decided to spend the winter at Fort Clark, both
McKenzie and Hamilton were disappointed for they were losing
a good companion who would have helped wile away the long bliz-
zards of winter. The party left Fort Union on October 31. The boat
stopped briefly at Fort William where Campbell gave them a part-
ing gift of cigars. The long summer sojourn would not be Maximilian's last contact with the American Fur Company. The very
next year, he would entertain Kenneth McKenzie at his German
estates.[32]

McKenzie's sudden decision to visit Europe seems to have been
based partly on a scandal of his making, a scandal that threatened the operations of the America Fur Company. In the summer
of 1832, the U.S. Government tightened the laws that prohibited
liquor in the Indian country. Long a staple of trade, liquor had
always found its way to the traders who felt it to be essential in
order to attract the Indians away from competitors, including the

29

British who did not prohibit it. In the fall of 1832, Crooks wrote a worried letter regretting "truly the blindness of the Government in refusing liquor . . . in the vicinity of the Hudson's Bay Posts."[33]

McKenzie was so alarmed by the prohibition that he made a personal visit to Washington in January 1833. When that failed, he cast about for some other means—in addition to the time-honored but risky smuggling that all traders had and would continue to carry out. By spring, he had concluded that while the laws prohibited the transportation of liquor they did not prohibit its manufacture in the Indian country. On the same steamboat that carried Prince Maximilian to Fort Union that summer rode McKenzie's brand new distillery.[34] Also on board was a supply of alcohol, but it was taken off when the boat was searched on the way up the river.[35]

McKenzie wrote Crooks in December 1833 telling him that Campbell and Sublette had succeeded in smuggling an abundance of alcohol. Crooks need not be alarmed, however, "For this post I have established a manufactory of strong water, it succeeds admirably. I have a good corn with a very respectable distillery and can produce as fine liquor as need be drank: I believe no law of the U.S. is hereby broken though perhaps one may be made to break up my distillery but liquor I must have or quit."[36]

Unknown to McKenzie, news of his still had already reached a rather wide circle of government officials and others. When McKenzie finally did learn that the secret was out, he blamed Nathaniel Wyeth.

Back in August, Wyeth, returning to the East overland after attempting to establish his own fur empire in the Pacific Northwest, stopped at Fort Union for three days. Wyeth was highly impressed with McKenzie, "all possible hospitality and politeness," by Hamilton, "a man of superior education and an Englishman," and by Fort Union, "better furnished inside than any British fort I have ever seen [including Fort Vancouver] at Table we have flour Bread Bacon Cheese Butter they live well.

Wyeth went on to say that "Fort Union is pleasantly situated on the N. bank of the Missouri. . . . I am told that there is not enough moisture here to raise vegetables potatoes grass ect." As he inspected the post, he saw "a small sturgeon but they are very rare Cat fish are good and plenty they have cows and bulls milk etc. I saw lime burning also [char]coal." He also saw the still, "here they are beginning to distil spirits from corn traded from the Inds.

below. This owing to some restrictions on the introduction of the article into the country."[37] Later, on November 11, back in Cambridge, Mass., Wyeth wrote a letter to the editor of a paper naming the many people who had treated him well on his expedition. Among the names was Kenneth McKenzie's.[38]

Nowhere in Wyeth's accounts can one find even a hint of his being displeased about his treatment while at Fort Union, or of his deliberately reporting McKenzie's still to the authorities. Yet, McKenzie blamed him, "in return for my civilities & furnishing him with a boat . . . on his arrival at Cant n. Leavenworth I hear he made some tremendous strong affidavits about my new manufactory."[39] Charles Larpenteur, who was to work for McKenzie, also thought it was Wyeth who told, as revenge for the exorbitant prices McKenzie charged him for supplies.[40]

However, Wyeth may have been blamed for something he did not do, or did not do alone. Travelling down the Missouri with him was none other than McKenzie's arch-rival, William Sublette.[41] The Indian Commissioner in Washington learned about the distillery from Henry L. Ellsworth, agent at Fort Leavenworth.[42] According to Ellsworth, he learned about the still from "a mountain trapper on his way down the Missouri." He went on, "Mr. Sublitz of St. Louis just from there [Fort Union], says, he tasted the whiskey made there, and found it an excellent quality."[43]

Federal officials gave serious thought to suspending the UMO's trading license. Pierre Chouteau, Jr., argued that the distillery was intended only "to promote the course of Botany." While the license was not suspended, Ramsay Crooks did not think the excuse to be very funny, **"prenez-y-garde**—Don't presume too much on your recent escape from an accusation, which might have been attended with serious consequences."[44]

Meanwhile, from the isolation of Fort Union, McKenzie, unaware that he had been experimenting in botany, came up with his own excuse, "An old acquaintance of mine in Red River Mr. J. P. Bourke addressed me last spring . . . in consequence whereof I purchased a still in St. Louis, & brought it hitherto & last fall he apprised me of his intention to come or send for it in April next." He again accused Wyeth of telling.[45]

The incident finally blew over. The friends of the American Fur Company, some of whom held high office, such as Secretary of War Lewis Cass, came to its assistance both in this and other incidents involving McKenzie and his associates.[46]

The location of the still in the fort cannot be established; however, Larpenteur mentioned the existence of a distillery house. This, of course, was not the end of the liquor trade; the company continued to smuggle alcohol in quantity. Larpenteur, the tee-totalling bartender, recounted, "The liquor business, which was always done at night, sometimes kept me up all night turning out drunken Indians, often by dragging them out by arms and legs."[47] As for McKenzie, upset by the buying out of Campbell and Sublette and the business of the still, 1834 seemed like a good time to leave the upper Missouri and to visit Europe.

A few miscellaneous entries in the records of the early 1830s add some detail to our understanding of the post. At the end of 1833, McKenzie noted that "the tin Smith arrived here Nov. 29. he is a good workman. I shall find him a most useful artisan."[48] There undoubtedly was some work for the tinsmith to do with regard to the fort itself; however, his most important job was making trade items such as bracelets, rings, and pots.

After McKenzie left on his vacation in 1834, Hamilton became the acting bourgeois. In September, he advised McKenzie by letter that one bastion was roofed, shingled, and pointed, and the other was built up as high as the pickets. This rather obscure news implies that either the two stone bastions were being rebuilt or Catlin and Bodmer had chosen to depict the fort as it would look, rather than as it did when they made their sketches.[49]

Hamilton continued his news by saying that Luteman (the head carpenter) had "made his arrangements for the kitchen," and had "erected and shingled five compartments, under the intended gallery." These compartments should not be confused with the range of apartments in which the clerks, interpreters, etc., lived; they were additional rooms built against the pickets and under a gallery that would eventually extend around the fort. He noted also the production of charcoal, "Michel has got 300 barrels of coal housed & his last kiln is now ready to draw."[50]

Three weeks later, Hamilton reported that (the stone mason?) "Miller has finished the bastions & starts today for St. Louis." Hamilton tried to get Miller to stay, but the latter asked for too much money and, besides, "his work is inferior in finish to Pow[der] Mag[azine]."[51]

After Pratte, Chouteau, and Company bought out Campbell and Sublette, McKenzie and Hamilton had Fort William on their hands. They moved all or part of the stockade from William to Union to

32

make the long-wanted corral for the horse herd. Larpenteur referred to this by writing, "Fort William was to be rebuilt within 150
yards of Union." The foreman for this project proved so incompe-
tent, according to Larpenteur, that "the pickets were set in crook-
ed, some too high, some too low." Larpenteur was then given the
job of superintendent; and he had the men take everything down,
straighten and level the trench, and start again. He succeeded in
building a respectable compound; at least he thought so.[52]

Although the pickets were moved up to Fort Union, the buildings
at Fort William remained where they were. In October 1834,
Larpenteur was selling drinks to a number of half-breeds, when
a violent argument broke out. During the fight, one of the
Deschampses killed another man. Larpenteur was able to quiet
things only by putting laudanum (opium) in their whiskey. When
the drunks recovered, they "went home to Fort William, where
all those families were kept, as were also some of the Company's
men who had squaws, and the horse guard with the horses."[53]

Setting Trap for Beaver, Alfred Jacob Miller, ca 1837. *Courtesy The InterNorth Art Found-
ation/Joslyn Art Museum, Omaha.*

As early as August 1832, John Jacob Astor had written that he feared "Beaver will not sell well very soon unless very fine, it . . . appears that they make hats of silk in place of Beaver."[54] This letter was Astor's admission that the heyday of the beaver trade (and the fabled mountain man) was drawing to a close. Silk was in fashion and, also, the beaver was fairly well trapped out. Beaver would continue to be an acceptable fur, along with the others; but as far as Fort Union was concerned, the buffalo, already important, would play an increasing role in the returns. McKenzie, in advice to one of his subordinates in January 1834, recognized this moment in the fur trade, "I am burdened with Apichemons [?], pieces of lodge & mean wolf skins, I must restrict you in the trade of those articles." Moreover, "dressed Cow skins should be traded only on very low terms. I have some thousand by me. Elk skins, Beaver skins & robes you cannot get too much of."[55]

The increasing importance of buffalo robes is pointed up by the references to them in the company correspondence. For example, Kipp wrote McKenzie in September 1834, without mentioning any other furs or skins, "Except to get as many buffalo robes as last year."[56]

John Jacob Astor, no longer a young man, felt no excitement in the change in emphasis from beaver to buffalo. As early as 1828, Pierre Chouteau, Jr., learned that Astor was contemplating selling his controlling interest in the American Fur Company.[57] The old man held out for six more years before retiring on June 1, 1834. Ramsay Crooks took over the Northern Department. Pratte, Chouteau, and Company bought out the Western Department. As far as the public was concerned, the term American Fur Company still applied to both. Crooks and Chouteau remained close business friends, and the extensive correspondence between them continued unabated. The UMO retained its special relationship to the St. Louis company; and, when he got back from his European jaunt, McKenzie returned up the Missouri to take charge of his empire.[58] Nevertheless, the future would be different than the past. Beaver was no longer king. Astor had grown old and had quit. There would be an exciting future for Fort Union, but it would reflect the changes taking place on the upper Missouri. As Tennyson would have it,

The old order changeth
Yielding place to new.

Notes

1. Chittenden, **American Fur Trade,** 1:329. Michael S. Kennedy, ed. **The Red Man's West** (New York: Hastings House, 1965), p.92.

2. Laidlaw, August 13, 1829, to Chouteau, Chouteau Papers, Wisconsin Historical Society. **Métis**—mixed blood, in this case usually of French Canadian and Indian descent. **Engagé** a laborer under contract. (Ramsay Crooks firmly believed that the best engagés were French Canadians.) **Mangeur du lard**—pork eater, anyone new in the fur trade in western waters.

3. Louis C. Butscher, "A Brief Biography of Prince Paul Wilhelm of Württemberg (1797-1860)," **New Mexico Historical Review** 17 (July 1972): 181-93, and "An Account of Adventures,"193-216 and 294-344. Prince Paul was a nephew of King Frederick I of Württemberg, Paul I of Russia, and (by marriage) Jerome Bonaparte; cousin to Nicholas I and Alexander I of Russia, Queen Victoria of England, and others. He made four trips to the United States, of which his one visit to Fort Union occurred during this second trip.

4. "Paul, Prince of Wirtembergh in Ac with Fort Union," Folder 1830, January-May, Chouteau Coll., MoHS.

5. **Ibid.**

6. William Backhouse Astor, March 30, 1833, to Pierre Chouteau, Jr., Folder 1833, March-April, Chouteau Coll., MoHS.

7. Pierre Jean DeSmet, S. J., **Life, Letter and Travels ... 1801-1873,** 4 vols. eds. H. M. Chittenden and A. T. Richardson (New York, 1905), 3:1132. DeSmet was not at Fort Union at this time; he heard the story from E. T. Denig and others.

8. Chittenden, **American Fur Trade,** 1:331-36.

9. McKenzie, February 4, 1832, to D. D. Mitchell, Folder 1832, January-February, Chouteau Coll., MoHS. McKenzie implied that the fire occurred on February 3. In the same letter, however, he wrote that five days had passed since the fire.

10. Chittenden, **American Fur Trade,** 1:103-09. Two thousand miles is a round figure. A U.S. Army Engineers survey in 1890 found the distance then to be 1,792 miles.

11. This is another of the several frustrations in dating major events at Fort Union. George Catlin said the boat arrived June 26. Chittenden has shown that the date was earlier by at least a few days. Chittenden, **American Fur Trade,** 1:339.

12. John Sanford was the technical owner of Dred Scott at the time of the latter's famous court case in 1856.

13. Audubon sprinkled his diary with criticisms of Catlin. Kurz said that Catlin was a "Yankee humbug," whose drawings were in bad taste.

14. Thomas Donaldson, **The George Catlin Indian Gallery in the U. S. National Museum.** Smithsonian Institution Report for 1885 (Washington: U.S. Government Printing Office, 1887), p.8, plate 5.

15. George Catlin, **A Descriptive Catalogue of Catlin's Indian Gallery** (London, 1840), p.36. Print no.388 shows the post. The original painting is in the Catlin Collection, Smithsonian Institution. In this same source, page 6, is a testimonial by Kenneth McKenzie as to the accuracy of Catlin's work.

16. John C. Ewers, "George Catlin, Painter of Indians and the West," **Annual Report ... of the Smithsonian Institution, 1955** (Washington: U.S. Government Printing office, 1956), p.493

17. Charles Larpenteur, **Forty Years a Fur Trader on the Upper Missouri, The Personal Narrative of Charles Larpenteur, 1833-1872,** ed. Elliott Coues (Minneapolis: Ross & Haines, 1962), 1:84 and 85n. Chittenden, **American Fur Trade,** 1:387.

18. George Catlin, **Letters and Notes on the ... North American Indians,** 2 vols. (London: Tilt and Bogue, 1842), 1:14 and 21-38. Later visitors supported Catlin's observations of the fort's operations, except for the 12-pounder. Denig reported in 1843 that the northeast bastion had one 3-pounder and one swivel gun; while the southwest bastion had but one swivel gun. See Audubon, 2:424.

19. Astor, September 28, 1832, to Pierre Chouteau, Jr., Astor Papers, vol.44, Baker Library, Harvard. Crooks, November 16, 1832, to Chouteau, Folder 1832, September-December, Chouteau Coll. MoHS.

20. Phillips, 2:424

21. Larpenteur, p.60. George R. Brooks, ed., "The Private Journal of Robert Camp-

bell," **The Bulletin, Missouri Historical Society** 20 (1963): 6-24 and 107-18. In this brief but valuable journal, Campbell gives many construction details. The pickets, rafted down the river, were eighteen feet long, hewn on one side, and averaging ten to twelve inches in diameter. Rock for the chimneys was found three miles from the fort. The roofs were covered with dirt. A rock-lined well, about twenty-five feet deep, was dug inside the stockade.

22. Hamilton, August 31, 1833, to Chouteau, Folder 1833, July-August, Chouteau Coll., MoHS.

23. Brooks, pp.22, 107, 108, and 115.

24. **Ibid.**, p.118.

25. McKenzie, January 31, 1834, to D. D. Mitchell, in Phillips, 2:425. See also McKenzie, December 13, 1833, to Kipp, Fort Union Letter Book, Chouteau Coll., MoHS.

26. Phillips, 2:428-29.

27. Brooks, p.8.

28. **Ibid.**, p.111.

29. Audubon, 2:181.

30. Brooks, p.8.

31. O. A. Stevens, "Maximilian in North Dakota, 1833-34," **North Dakota History** 28 (1961):163-64. Abel, p.235, n110.

32. Reuben Gold Thwaites, ed., **Early Western Travels**, vols.22-25 (Cleveland: The Arthur H. Clark Co., 1906). Volumes 22-24 contain Maximilian's travels; volume 25 has Bodmer's drawings. For this account, see 22:373-88, 23:11-27 and 188-207, and 24:317. Hamilton, October 29, 1833, to Kipp, Fort Union Letter Book, Chouteau Coll., MoHS.

33. Crooks, November 16, 1832, to Chouteau, Folder 1832, September-December, Chouteau Coll., MoHS.

34. Phillips, 2:426.

35. McKenzie, December 16, 1833, to W. B. Astor, Fort Union Letter Book, Chouteau Coll., MoHS.

36. **Ibid**. See also in the same source McKenzie, December 16, 1833, to Joshua Pilcher.

37. F. G. Young, ed., "The Correspondence and Journals of Captain Nathaniel J. Wyeth, 1831-6," **Sources of the History of Oregon**, vol.1, parts 3-6 (Eugene, 1899), p.212.

38. **Ibid.**, p.79.

39. McKenzie, January 21, 1834, to Mitchell, Fort Union Letter Book, Chouteau Coll., MoHS.

40. Larpenteur, 1:74.

41. While Chittenden, **American Fur Trade,** 1:446, says this was Milton Sublette, William's brother, it would seem that it was William, who went down about this time because of illness. I have found no record of Milton being in the area.

42. Ellsworth went on to become the first U.S. Commissioner of Patents and is called the "father" of the Department of Agriculture. Allen Johnson, ed., **Dictionary of American Biography**, 20 vols. (New York: Charles Scribner's Sons, 1943), 6:110-11.

43. Ellsworth, November 8, 1833, to E. Herring, Indian Commissioner, Indians Collection, MoHS.

44. Crooks, February 23, 1834, to Chouteau, Folder 1834, January-March, Chouteau Coll., MoHS.

45. McKenzie, March 18, 1834, to Chouteau, Fort Union Letter Book, Chouteau Coll., MoHS.

46. Porter, 2:769-70.

47. Larpenteur, 1:74-76.

48. McKenzie, December 15, 1833, to H. Picotte, and December 10, 1835, to M. Belhumeux.

49. Hamilton, September 17, 1834, to McKenzie, Fort Union Letter Book, Chouteau Coll., MoHS.

50. **Ibid.**

51. **Ibid.**, October 9, 1834.

52. Larpenteur, **Forty Years**, 1:77-78. Charles Larpenteur, "Journals,"1:1834-37, Minnesota Historical Society. In 1837, Larpenteur wrote that Indians "got over the pickets of the old fort" in an attempt to steal the horses.

53. Larpenteur, **Forty Years,** 1:77-78.

54. Astor, August 1832, to Chouteau, Folder 1832, June-August, Chouteau Coll., MoHS.

55. McKenzie, January 8, 1834, to Sam Tulloch, Fort Union Letter Book, Chouteau Coll., MoHS.

56. Kipp, September 5, 1834, to McKenzie, Folder 1834, September-December, Chouteau Coll., MoHS.

57. Crooks, November 18, 1828, to Chouteau, Folder 1828, August-December, Chouteau Coll., MoHS.

58. W. B. Astor, December 31, 1834, to Chouteau, Folder 1834, September-December, Chouteau Coll., MoHS. Chittenden, **American Fur Trade**, 1:365.

CHAPTER 4

From Beaver to Buffalo

Charles Larpenteur's self-righteous sobriety undoubtedly brought him into conflict with his fellow employees from time to time. Nevertheless, he is more valuable historically than most of the other men at the fort, for he kept a diary rather than get drunk. His detailed journal shows that while Fort Union was six years old in 1835, it was by no means "finished."

Larpenteur held McKenzie in considerable awe, which feeling was increased the first time he entered the dining room. He discovered that clerks, who ate at the head table, had to wear their coats to meals. Moreover, no one could eat until McKenzie was seated; since McKenzie was a late riser, this meant that breakfast was not eaten until nine o'clock. Still, it was worth the wait:

> On entering the eating hall, I found a splendidly set table with a very white tablecloth, and two waiters, one a negro. Mr. McKenzie was sitting at the head of the table, extremely well dressed. The victuals consisted of fine fat buffalo meat, with plenty of good fresh butter, cream, and milk . . . but I saw that only two biscuits were allowed to each one, as these were placed at each plate. I soon discovered, by the manner in which the clerks took their seats, that mine would come very near the end of the table, for it appeared to go by grade.[1]

He did not say whether or not Hamilton modified the dining ritual during McKenzie's absence in Europe. By going abroad, McKenzie missed the very wet summer of 1835, "The quantity of rain which has fallen here this season I should think is almost without precedent." The woods became swamps, grass grew abundantly everywhere, the interior of the fort became a lake, and the mosquitoes came in clouds, making "the men cry out terribly and not without cause."[2]

Back in September 1834, Hamilton had noted that the bastions were well along toward completion. He confirmed this in March 1835 by writing, "The Bastions are completed with the exception of laying down the floors but the planks are all tongue and grooved." Other construction activities at this time were mentioned in the rather cryptic note, "Laucier was employed untill Christmas in finishing the attics." Also, timber had been got out for new storerooms, the existing ones being only temporary in nature.[3]

Luteman started work on the framing for the "stores and warehouses" on May 1. From time to time his assistants were called away to other jobs, but he worked steadily on this job. On May 15 and 25, the drivers hauled rocks for the building's foundation; other men were kept busy sawing timber. Work slowed down when the rains came, such as the afternoon, "about three o'clock a heavy thunder storm . . . the fort yard like a lake."

On May 28, Luteman reached the point where he had to pull the old building down to make room for the new. For the next three days the men moved the supplies from the old structure. The goods in the storerooms were carried to the bastions, while those in the retail store were moved to "the Northwest end room of Mr. McKenzie's Dwelling house." In order to speed up the work, "the Drivers made a Bridge across a ravine to enable them to make four loads of rocks per day instead of three." This ravine may have been "Garden Coulee," one-half mile east of the fort.

By June 2, the carpenter had finished the framing, which work had been done to one side. The next day, nine workmen "commenced pulling down the [old] store & ware houses." Meanwhile, a second carpenter began constructing the door and window frames, and four men were "sawing planks for sheeting the new buildings." Four days later the old buildings were out of the way, as was a "part of the stables which was in the way of the new buildings." (From Denig's description a few years later, these stables were probably located against the palisade.) At this point, the old sills were

40

hauled away and "Holmes and Kieffer diging the foundations for the new building."

For the next few days a variety of jobs were carried on: framing rafters, constructing the foundations, hauling in lime and sand and hauling out earth, making shingles, and hauling in the new sills. Finally, on June 19, all hands "commenced raising the buildings."

In four days the framing was complete. To celebrate, the men "tied a [posey?] on the top of one of the rafters and fired [a] few guns towards it with the view of gitting [a treat?] which is commonly done in such occasions and was administered to them to their satisfaction." Luteman, "who is the boss carpenter received a bottle . . . which induced him to get in a spree." He was still sick the next day, and the work was temporarily reduced to two men straightening the edges of shingles.

The next steps were to sheet the roof and to put five men to work digging the cellar. At the same time rock quarrying was renewed for lining the cellar walls. The earth removed from the cellar was spread on the fort yard in an attempt to give it a gradual slope toward the river so that it would drain. On July 1, Luteman finished sheeting the building and commenced shingling the roof. Hamilton wrote McKenzie that "the new stores are in part shingled and have a very imposing appearance. We are short of 10 dy and 12 dy cut nails."[4] A week later, Holmes finished digging the cellar and began its stone wall, while another man started putting in the window and door frames. Two men worked at putting tongues and grooves in the floor boards. The only things remaining to be done were weatherboarding the walls and planking the floor.

In early September, Larpenteur was able to record that the supplies in the bastions were being put in the new warehouses and that the men were storing potatoes in the new cellar. On September 24, two men were directed to paint the roof red; however, they ran out of paint with only one-quarter of the roof covered.[5]

To complement Larpenteur's description of the construction of the building was Edwin Denig's description of it that he prepared in 1843:

> On the east side of the fort, extending north and south, is a building, or range, all under one roof, 127 ft. long by 25 ft. deep, and used for the following purposes. A small room at the north end for stores and luggage; then the retail store . . . where all white persons buy or sell . . . . Adjoining this is the wholesale warehouse, in which

is kept the principal stock of goods intended for the extensive trade, this room is 57 ft. in length. Next is a small room for the storage of meat and other supplies. At the end is the press room, where all robes, furs, the peltries are stored. The dimensions [of this room] extend to the top of the roof inside, which roof is perfectly waterproof. It will contain from 2800 to 3000 packs of Buffalo robes [10 robes to the pack]. All this range is very strongly put together, weather-boarded outside, and lined with plank within. It has also cellar and garet.[6]

The cellar depression may still be seen, but nothing else of this structure remains above ground. Still, it would seem that Luteman deserved his bottle—and perhaps a second—for a job well done.

A multitude of other projects were completed that muddy summer. Larpenteur's journal for May and June does not indicate clearly if the milk house underwent a renovation or was brand new. At any rate, men worked on its underpinning, "paved" its interior, shingled the roof, made a new window and a new door frame and door, and plastered and whitened its interior walls. The kitchen, located behind the bourgeois's house, also had its floor paved. The Indian house, located west of the main (south) gate also underwent repairs. Some iron stored in it was removed to the southwest bastion, and the room was cleaned up so that the men could store packs of robes in it. The roof of the Indian house was covered at this time with lodge skins, which in turn were covered with earth. Larpenteur wrote that the workmen "dried the lodges which covered the Indian house and recovered it again to remain untill the Packs are taken out."

Minor jobs around the fort included "sawing old logs about the Fort for fire wood"; "working at the May Pole to hoist the Flag," which pole was not raised until May 3; "hauling rails and shingle wood from the other Fort [William] for Baptiste Marcham to make shingles of"; repairing the chimneys at Fort William, where some of the fort families were living; "hauling lime and sand to plaster the Clerks room"; "hauling sawlogs to the saw pit"; constructing a calf pen with the puncheons removed from the old warehouse; making a calf shed; repairing the earthen roof of the ice house; rendering tallow; "haulling earth to fille up the yard before the ice house"; removing all the robe packs out of "the room next to the Clerks in order to have it clear for the free [not under contract] trappers"; manufacturing a wheel barrow and an axel tree; bail-

42

ing the water out of the just completed milk house; and hauling gravel into the fort's yard.

Still other jobs included hauling wood to the charcoal pit; "pointing the under pining of the sills around the outside of the Fort"; planting four cedar posts on the river bank for tying the boats to; "John Prill raking the [buffalo?] chips off the bank on front of the Fort into the river, then graduating the river bank and making steps leading down to the water"; mowing and hauling hay; "splighting the fire wood smaller and piling it between the kitchen and the Dwelling house"; making an enclosure for a stockyard with timbers from the old warehouse; underpinning the gallery sills; repairing the chimneys; making and bundling up shingles for future use; making oars; cutting timber suitable for making ax handles; making a new saw pit on the south side of the river; building a canoe (hollowing out a log?); building new stables under the galleries; and putting in an upper floor in the men's apartments. Another undertaking of interest involved the inside of the office, where a workman put rocks "next to the weather boarding between the studing in order to be plaistered over."

In contrast to earlier attempts, a garden thrived in the rains of 1835. The first seeds, planted on May 11, included potatoes, corn, peas, red onions, radishes, lettuce, parsnips, carrots, yellow French radishes, celery, curled parsley, oyster plant, "and a mixture of seeds supposed to be turnip seed." Larpenteur, who apparently had some responsibility for the garden, mentioned two growing areas: a vegetable garden in or near to Garden Coulee and a field of sorts across the river. He was quite specific about the planting of corn, squash, pumpkin, watermelon, and beets on the south bank. Also planted in one or the other of the sites were onions, cabbages, cucumbers, dwarf beans, and pole beans.

A fence was erected around the garden and a "walk" laid. By June 5, the first radishes were "fit to eat"; a few days later John Prill began "cutting pea sticks." A small, third area was planted on June 12 when Larpenteur "sewed radishes and Tongue grass in the Distilling house yard." A particularly bad rain on June 19 washed away eight "panels" of the garden fence and it took two men a day to repair it. Another emergency occurred on August 26 when a number of Indians arrived: "Imployed all hands in diging the Potatoes...and was obliged to pull the corn green...for at the rate the Indians were gathering it they would not have left one ear by morning."

Nevertheless, 1835's gardening was a success. Hamilton, in a burst of optimism, sent a substantial order for seeds to St. Louis for the following year.[7] That fall, after the last vegetable had been gathered, the Indians began burning the fence rails. Larpenteur was forced to have two carters haul all the fencing to the protection of the fort.

He did not write much about the domestic animals at Fort Union, except for the hogs. Several adventures happened to the pigs, such as the terse entry, "Killed seven dogs for having torn the hogs to pieces." The herd was reinforced later when "John Prill brought in a sow from the woods with five young pigs." This increase was diminished when "one of the old sows choked her self with a piece of meat."

McKenzie was not at Fort Union during the summer when the deeds of the Deschamps family caught up with the father and sons. Exiles from the Red River Settlement, they had drifted toward the upper Missouri where Campbell had hired them at Fort William. When Campbell discovered that François Deschamps, Jr., was secretly a spy for McKenzie, François deserted to Fort Union where he was employed as an interpreter. Both he and his father, François, Sr., tried the temper of their fellow employees many times. A particularly strong feud developed between them and Baptiste Gardepied, whose life they repeatedly threatened. Baptiste finally demanded a showdown. The result took place in Larpenteur's room when Baptiste wounded François, Jr., and killed the old man. For a while thereafter the surviving Deschampes caused very little trouble for anyone.[8]

Another moment of excitement recorded by Larpenteur involved the arrival of a number of Indians who were allowed to stay in the fort. Possibly because of liquor, the Indians became so unruly that Hamilton became concerned. He directed Larpenteur to carry muskets from a bastion to the dining room and to put a small cannon in the hallway of the bourgeois's house. Then, "the window blinds of the dining room were opened, and there could be seen by the three candles the bright muskets, plenty of cartridges . . . and four men ready for action. The piece of artillery was rolled back and forward in the passage, making a tremendous noise, and two men mounted guard with muskets and fixed bayonets." This display of power quieted the visitors; and a very pleased Hamilton sent Larpenteur to the cellar to draw a bottle of Madeira for a celebration.[9]

44

Another Indian whose name entered the history of Fort Union in 1835 was La Main, an Assiniboin who had had several disputes with his own people and who was thought of as an outlaw. In the early 1830s, he had killed his half-brother, Broken Cloud, at the fort; and, now, another half-brother got revenge by shooting La Main and leaving his body to tumble into the fort when the gates were opened the next morning.[10]

All in all, 1835 was a busy, exciting year, so busy that on July 4, Larpenteur wrote, "hollow day but had very little time to enjoy it." Yet there were times when the men relaxed a little. In the cool of the evenings, especially, there was time to promenade on the gallery that ran around the fort. From here one could see the prairie, the river, and the fiery sunsets and dream a little about home or the mountains.

Back in May 1834, Hamilton had hoisted the flag and fired the guns to honor the departure of McKenzie. Now, word arrived that McKenzie was planning to remain in St. Louis. It was a premature rumor. He returned in late fall 1835 to renew his control over the fur trade of the upper Missouri. From Fort Union he wrote Prince Maximilian thanking him for the hospitality on the Rhine. He also mentioned the bad news that the steamboat that had carried the prince's collection of mammal and bird specimens had sunk with the loss of all the cargo. As for McKenzie's own trip, it had been a good one, with a side visit to Niagara Falls on the way home. The river was already frozen; but McKenzie looked forward to the winter. There was Hamilton for company. Still, he asked, would the prince kindly think of Fort Union from time to time.[11]

The year 1836 was, perhaps, the quietest year Fort Union had yet experienced. The trade in robes was steady. Liquor was smuggled in. The Indians came and went. The next year started out just as quietly. Edwin Denig wrote in March 1837 to Fort Pierre, sending his thanks for the letters and papers that had just arrived, "we were beginning to get mere drones for the want of news." He said that nearly everyone at the fort had been sick with something like influenza, from which one child had died. On the other hand, trade had been superior, "We now have 900 packs in the warehouse and at least 250 more to be traded, and all of the very best kind of robes." He exulted, "if we make 2500 Packs Hurray for Upper Missouri Outfit against the world!!"

Despite the influenza, morale was high, "We are all in good humor . . . every man attends his business well and Mr. McKenzie is kind and obliging to all." As for himself, Denig said he "would rather be ostler here than bookkeeper general at F[ort] P[ierre] and though to oblige and obey Mr. McKenzie I would go any place, yet should I leave here it would be with great regret."[12] McKenzie, however, left Fort Union in 1837 to take up residency in St. Louis.

Three months after Denig wrote his letter, Fort Union's high spirits were replaced by the darkest gloom. The steamer **St. Peters** brought the smallpox with it. The first person to take ill was the acting bourgeois, Jacob Halsey. Within a few days, twenty-seven people lay sick within the fort, of whom four died. Larpenteur described the desperation felt, "Doctor Thomas Medical Book was brought down from the Library and the treatment of small Pox vaccination noculation was read over and over." The Assiniboins kept coming in to trade even though efforts were made to stop them. Like a wild fire, the pox spread through the tribe, and most of the other tribes of the upper Missouri. The Indians had no resistance to the disease. Halsey estimated that about ten out of twelve Indians who caught the disease would die.[13]

The loss was terrible. The Mandan Indians were almost completely killed off. D. D. Mitchell, at Fort Union, estimated that four-fifths of the Assinboins and the Blackfeet had died.[14] Buffalo were plentiful that year, but there were few Indians to hunt them. The American Fur Company worried that the Indians would blame the company for the disaster and attack the forts. Indeed, one Assiniboin leader, Le Vieux Gauche, vowed his vengeance on Union. Halsey took the threat seriously and had a double gate put in at the main entrance. The outside gates could then be opened, the Indians could come through them and enter the Indian house; providing the inner gates were closed, the Indians could not come into the main part of the fort. As a further precaution, a wicket was added to the wall. Larpenteur used it when selling liquor to visiting Indians. He said a few shots were fired through it from time to time, but these were caused by the liquor, not by a desire for revenge.[15]

Hamilton, who had gone down to St. Louis with McKenzie, compiled the "melancholy details" from the upper forts and passed the dire news on to Pierre Chouteau, Jr., then in Washington. He confirmed most of Halsey's reports; he also noted that Halsey had done a poor job at Fort Union that summer. The new acting bourgeois, D. D. Mitchell, had written asking that Chouteau himself come up to settle a number of unnamed problems; he also gave "a woeful picture of poor Halsey's conduct during the summer."[16]

Despite the tragedy, the robe trade continued, slowly for a time but gradually increasing in volume again.[17] Fort Union continued to witness small excitements among its inhabitants. In 1840, one George Sumpter robbed the retail store and got away, only to be found working at Fort Pierre two years later. He was promptly "set adrift." The Deschampses were replaced in character by Alexander Harvey, a capable person possessed of a violent temper. He was fired in 1839, then rehired a year later. He returned to Fort Union where he had a showdown with an old enemy, Isadore Sandoval, in the same store that Sumpter robbed. In the manner of the upper Missouri, Harvey shot and killed Sandoval and dared anyone to do anything about it.[18]

In counterpoise to this violence, Pierre DeSmet, the Jesuit missionary, made this year the first of many visits to Fort Union.[19] Like other travelers, he was impressed with "the vastest and finest of the forts that the Fur Company has upon the Missouri." True to company policy, James Kipp, the new bourgeois, and his employees "overwhelmed us with civilities. . . . supplied all our wants . . . I shall be most thankful to them all my life." He performed no marriages, but "regenerated sundry half-breed children in the holy waters of baptism" before pushing on down the Missouri.[20]

When DeSmet made his next visit, in 1842, Fort Union had neighbors again. A new competitor, called both the Union Fur Company and Fox, Livingston and Company, established a post at or near the site of old Fort William. Although officially called Fort Mortimer by its owners, the old name "William" remained popular. The new post was first built of wood, including its walls. Later, either under Fox, Livingston and Company or under still another competitor, it was rebuilt with adobe, the first time such material was used that far up the Missouri.

The new fort got off to a poor start. In 1843, a sudden and very high rise in the Yellowstone river cut into the north bank of the junction. Even as the occupants watched, the bank collapsed right up to the fort's walls. Working desperately, they succeeded in moving the front wall and the buildings nearest the water back so that "the back buildings of the Fort as it was before the rise now are the Front ones."[21]

Like Campbell and Sublette, the Union Fur Company found it impossible to compete profitably with Fort Union. Although Kenneth McKenzie was not on the river, his successor as chief agent,

Alexander and Natawistacha (Medicine Snake Woman) Culbertson and their son, Joe, ca 1863. Alexander Culbertson was an outstanding trader on the Upper Missouri. He joined the American Fur Company in 1833. He served as bourgeois at Forts McKenzie and Union. He built Fort Benton. In the 1840s and '50s he was the company's general manager of the UMO. Mrs. Culbertson was the attractive daughter of a Blackfoot chief and was of considerable assistance to her husband during negotiations with Indians. *Courtesy Montana Historical Society, Helena.*

Alexander Culbertson, was a most worthy heir. Fort Mortimer held out against him for three years but, in 1845, the Union Fur Company gave up and sold its few holdings to Pierre Chouteau, Jr., and Company.[22]

Master Captain Joseph A. Sire could not bring his steamboat, the **Omega**, quite up to the landing at Fort Union in 1843. A sandbar lay in the way. He could take satisfaction, however, that he had made the fastest trip yet—St. Louis to Fort Union in forty-eight days and seven hours.[23] His passengers were quite impressed. On board was a party of five men led by John James Audubon, then about sixty years old. With him were his long-time friend and amateur ornithologist, wealthy Edward Harris, John G. Bell, Lewis M. Squires, and Isaac Sprague, a 32-year-old artist whose job it was to draw plants and backgrounds for Audubon's fauna.[24] From this group came a number of letters, at least three diaries, and two paintings of Fort Union, and from this wealth of material came a detailed picture of life at the fourteen-year-old fort that summer.[25]

Fort and steamboat exchanged salutes, firing six guns for the occasion. To welcome the visitors, "the gentlemen of the fort came down on horseback, and appeared quite a cavalcade." The guests met Culbertson, then walked to the fort where they "drank some first-rate port wine." They returned to the steamboat for the night, and not until the next day was their luggage "taken to the landing of the fort in a large keel boat."[26]

Isaac Sprague, a member of John James Audubon's party in 1843, sketched Fort Union from across the Missouri River. The stone bastions appear to be whitewashed. To the right of the fort, the faint outline of a corral built of palisades from Fort William may be seen. One suspects the skiff is the one identified in inventories as worth $5. *Courtesy National Audubon Society, New York.*

Audubon was quite disappointed at the small, dark, dirty room, about twelve by fourteen feet, with only one window, on the west side, that was given to the party, now increased to six."[7] When he learned that this was the room that Maximilian had used, he could hardly believe it. However, he was but a guest and decided not to complain. The six men turned in early that first night, hoping to get a good rest. No sooner had they gone to bed, when a drunk in the room above them began cursing loudly. All lay awake, hoping the drunk would fall asleep, but now "clarionets, fiddles, and a drum were heard in the dining room" next door to their room. This new noise caused the drunk to renew his swearing "as if quite fresh."

When an invitation to join the party arrived, Squires jumped out of bed, investigated, and returned with the information that a ball was in progress. The rest got up to attend the dance:

Several squaws, attired in their best, were present, with
all their guests, engages, clerks, etc. Mr. Culbertson

played the fiddle very fairly; Mr. Guépe the clarionet, and
Mr. Chouteau [probably Pierre Chouteau, Jr.'s, half-breed
nephew] the drum. . . . Cotillions and reels were
danced . . . and the company dispersed about one o'clock.
We retired for the second time, and now occurred a dispute
between the drunkard and another man; but . . . I was
so wearied that I fell asleep.

Audubon still did not complain about the quarters. However, the
strain must have showed on his face. The next day Culbertson offered them a larger and quieter room upstairs in the bourgeois's
house.[28]

As they became acquainted with the fort and its surroundings,
Audubon and his friends made a number of references to various
structures and landmarks. No attempt is made to weave these into a chronological narrative. Audubon was favorably impressed
with the dining room fare, "We have bread only twice a day, morning and evening, but we have very excellent Milk, and Butter, and
probably the best Catfish found in the World." He noticed the "pig's
trough, which is immediately under the side of the fort," but made
it no clearer whether the pigs were housed inside or outside the
palisades. He made reference to a bell ringing at sunrise; it was
the signal to open the gate. However, Sprague's sketches do not
show the bell tower that appears in paintings done several years
later.

One day, fourteen warriors arrived, their faces painted black to
show that they were a war party. They were allowed to stay in
the Indian house just inside the front gate. Culbertson, however,
took their drum away because of the noise. Later, another group
of Assiniboins were allowed to spend the night in the space between the outer and inner gates. During the night they built a large
fire in that small space; Audubon thought it "a wonder that the
whole establishment was not destroyed by fire."

Sprague's drawings indicate that the bourgeois's house was still
only one and one-half stories high. However, Denig's description
of that year stated there was a porch. Also, Denig made reference
to Audubon and Squires sleeping on the porch during a hot spell.

When Larpenteur described the building of the new storerooms
in 1835, he made many references to the carters hauling rock.
Audubon mentioned planning to go to the quarry "from which the
stones for the powder magazine were brought." This quarry probably was the one for which a bridge was built back in the 1830s

to allow the carters to speed their operations.

Audubon also confirmed that the fort still operated a "ferry flat" large enough to carry a cart across the river. On one occasion, he went across with a cart and drove on "an old abandoned road, filled with fallen timber and bushes" on the south side. The reference to fallen timber supports Catlin's painting which shows a great deal of timber on the south shore, an area that is open, cultivated land today.

Both Audubon and Sprague referred to six-pounders at the fort firing salutes to departing mackinaws and keel boats. Denig at this time mentioned only three-pounders. Audubon further complicated this matter when he described the departure of Chardon for the Blackfoot country, "The flag of Fort Union was hoisted, the four pounder ran out of the front gate. . . . The keel boat had a brass swivel on her bows, and fired first, then off went the larger gun."

Also contradictory were Audubon's references to the garden. As it had been in the lush summer of 1835, the garden was located in the coulee one-half mile east of the fort. In this year, gardeners had much trouble from stealing by the employees of Fort Mortimer. Audubon said this stealing became so bad the garden was abandoned. But, later, he told of Crees pulling up squash vines and turnips and tearing down the pickets around the garden. Apparently there were some vegetables left, for "we all turned to, and picked a quantity of peas, which with a fine roast pig, made us a capital dinner."

One day, Audubon and some companions went for a walk in the hills just north of the fort: "From the top of the hills we saw a grand panorama of a most extensive wilderness, with Fort Union beneath us and far away, as well as the Yellowstone River, and the lake across the river. The hills across the Missouri appeared quite low, and we could see the high prairie beyond, forming the background." The view is very much the same today.[29]

One adventure of Audubon's at Fort Union badly misfired. He was desirous of acquiring an Indian's skull and persuaded Edwin Denig to help him remove one from an Indian scaffold burial. The two of them set off on the morning of July 2 "with a bag and instruments, to take off the head of a three-years-dead Indian Chief." They succeeded in removing the head, but they could not get the coffin back up in the tree. Somewhat shaken, they buried everything.[30]

Turning to Harris's journal, we find still more descriptive

Assiniboin tree burials as depicted by Karl Bodmer, 1833. *Courtesy Smithsonian Institution National Anthropological Archives.*

material. When he first saw the fort, he wrote that it was "constructed on a plan similar to the others, excepting that the logs which, in others, are planted in the ground were framed, on a stone foundation, as to form a gallery from which a besieged party may fire over the ramparts at the enemy. The building and appointments throughout are," he thought, "of a description superior to any Fort we have seen on the river."

Nearly all the forts along the Missouri had a **chantier**, or boatyard, usually located in a suitable growth of timber. Here the workmen built mackinaws, skiffs, and canoes for river transportation. The chantier at Fort Union seems to have changed from time to time as suitable timber was exhausted at any one point. In 1843, it appears that the boats (a mackinaw and a skiff were under construction) were built right at Fort Union. The timber came from the woods across the river. This arrangement came to light when Harris described the mysterious disappearance of the scow used for crossing the river. "This is a serious loss," he wrote, "particularly at this time as they are very busy in building and fitting out the Mackinaw boat for Mr. Kipp to ascend the Yellowstone to the Crow establishment . . . they also have a skiff building for our use, and the men have to cross the river two or three times a day to work out the timber in the woods." Also crossing the river daily were men who were burning charcoal on the south side for the blacksmith.

Harris took a great interest in the condition of the competitor, Fort Mortimer. When a Mr. Collins there became ill, Harris visited him regularly, acting the role of "doctor." On one occasion he took Audubon with him, the two of them riding down in Fort Union's carryall. Conditions at Mortimer were miserable after the flooding of the Yellowstone. The rain beat into the shanty where Collins was trying to recover, and the fort had virtually run out of food.

Harris also spent much of his time exploring the countryside. Once, when riding in the vicinity of "Garden river," he spotted a wolf. He also visited "Wormwood Prairie,"one and one-half miles above the fort to the west, where in good years (such as 1843), the men mowed hay, "It is a beautiful bottom prarie [sic] covered with a sort of blue-stemmed grass said to be of the best quality." Harris and Bell spent July 4 deer hunting in a ravine leading off from this prairie to the north. On another occasion, Larpenteur took Harris and Audubon on a wagon trip to some sandstone hills about two miles north of the fort. They spent some time looking for fossils, but without success.[31]

Of the three diarists, Isaac Sprague was easily the most enthusiastic about the strange and wonderful way of life of the fur traders, although, worried about his health, he held back from full participation in it. He had barely arrived when Culbertson performed a dramatic pursuit. When someone spotted a wolf running across the prairie, Culbertson "immediately mounted his horse and proceeded in pursuit of him. In a very short time he came up with him and shot him while running at full speed, and in less than 20 minutes the wolf was brought into the fort."

Another feat that impressed Sprague was a demonstration by the better riders and shots of the fort: "Several of them rode out about ¾ of a mile from the fort starting from thence with unloaded guns, and while running that short distance at full speed they managed to load and fire from 9 to 11 times." With admiration, he wrote, "The horses are guided by inclining the body to either side, the reins being thrown loose upon the neck, leaving both hands free to use the gun."

His respect for Culbertson no doubt increased when the bourgeois presented the painter with "a beautiful Indian dress consisting of a Shirt Leggins and Mantle all of which are made of skins of various animals and highly ornamented with porcupine quills pieces of shells etc." He noted that July 4 passed without a celebration, a situation that appears to have occurred more often than not at Fort Union. A few days later, he visited the place about one mile from the fort where the Assiniboins placed their dead on scaffolds. After that, he crossed the river to sketch his views of Fort Union from the south side.

At least once more during the summer, Culbertson showed off for his visitors' pleasure. One afternoon, he, Owen McKenzie (the halfbreed son of Kenneth McKenzie), and none other than Squires, "arranged in Indian Costume, accompanied by two Blackfeet squaws in native dress made a grand display on horseback. They performed a number of evolutions on the prairie, and rode to the hills where they espied a wolf to which they gave chase and shot—and after returned to the fort at full speed." What a time to live! What a place to be!

Sprague was fascinated by the sight of Indians eating buffalo; they "eat the brain, the inner coat of the nostrils, etc. raw!" They also ate raw the liver and the stomach lining, or tripe. Sprague tried the latter, "but did not relish it much. Though I could eat it about as well as any tripe."

As his days at Fort Union grew short in number, Sprague became philosophical. Concerning the fort's employees, "Here far from civilization, the traders pass the best of their days—some from a Love of adventure some for gain—and other for crime are driven from civilized society." He doubted if he would ever meet any of them again.[32]

Before he left Fort Union, Audubon persuaded the post's book-keeper, Edwin Thompson Denig, to write a description of the establishment. Denig put down in 2,000 words the most complete description of the post known to exist. Although several important changes occurred in the fort's appearance after 1843, Denig's description remains a basic document. Audubon possibly agreed with Denig's thought that the fur traders did indeed "enjoy at least the semblance of living like their more quiet, though not more useful brothers in the United States."[33]

Kenneth McKenzie returned to Fort Union in the autumn of 1844. It was not a pleasure trip nor a journey of reminiscences. Persuaded by Pierre Chouteau, Jr., that affairs on the upper Missouri were so bad, because of mismanagement (particularly because of Francis Chardon's firing a cannon at a group of Indians who had come to Fort McKenzie to trade), as to need his attention, McKenzie had reluctantly agreed to leave his wife and business to spend the winter of 1844-45 on the upper Missouri. Unfortunately, no record of this stop at Fort Union has been uncovered. He wrote his wife from Fort Pierre, October 27, that "in a few days . . . we will start again for Fort Union at the mouth of the Yellow Stone River." Later, in an effort to settle his accounts with the company, he stated that "at great inconvenience, & loss to his private affairs, [he] . . . visited the trading posts . . . for the purpose of examining into the Company's affairs there, and of pacifying the Indians." He had no doubts about the success of his trip, "after spending some seven months there so occupied, he left the country in a peaceable state, and the trade revived & prosperous." For this task, McKenzie asked reimbursement to the tune of ten thousand dollars. He was no longer the king of the upper Missouri, but there was still a good deal about him that was princely in nature.[34]

Notes

1. Larpenteur, **Forty Years**, 1:70-71.

2. Abel, p.300, n.371, quoting Hamilton, July 17, 1835.

3. Hamilton, March 29, 1835, to McKenzie, Fort Union Letter Book, Chouteau Coll., MoHS.

4. **Ibid,** July 4, 1835.

5. Larpenteur, "Journals,"1834-37.

6. Audubon, 2:183-84. During the 1830s, Fort Union had a screw-type fur press. In later years, it had a large robe press outside its walls.

7. Hamilton, July 17, 1835, to Daniel Lamont, Fort Union Letter Book, Chouteau Coll., MoHS.

8. Larpenteur, **Forty Years**, 1:87-90. Hamilton, August 25, 1835, to Laidlaw, Folder 1835, January-December, Chouteau Coll., MoHS. A year or so later, a one-day civil war broke out between the Deschamps family on one side and most of the employees of Fort Union on the other. The Deschampses holed up in the old buildings at Fort William. McKenzie, on demand, let his men take a small cannon for their attack. By the end of the day, all the Deschampses were dead, from either bullets or fire, and several of Fort William's buildings lay in ashes.

9. Larpenteur, **Forty Years**, 1:83-84. No other reference to this incident has been found.

10. DeSmet, 3:1183. DeSmet was led to believe that a double gate existed at this time. Actually, it was not built until 1837.

11. McKenzie, December 10, 1835, to Prince Maximilian, Fort Union Letter Book, Chouteau Coll., MoHS.

12. Denig, March 25, 1837, to Jacob Halsey, Folder 1837, June-July, Chouteau Coll., MoHS.

13. Abel, pp.394-96. Larpenteur, **Forty Years**, 1:183-87. Halsey, November 2, 1837, "Report on Small-Pox Epidemic," for Pratte, Chouteau & Co., Folder 1837, July-December, Chouteau Coll., MoHS.

14. Mitchell, December 1, 1837, to Papin, Folder 1837, July-December, Chouteau Coll.,MoHS.

15. Abel, p.396. Larpenteur, 1:135.

16. Hamilton, February 25, 1838, to Pierre Chouteau, Jr., Folder 1838, January-February, Chouteau Coll., MoHS. This letter also contains a description of the effects of the smallpox on the various tribes and bands on the upper Missouri. According to Chittenden, **American Fur Trade**, 1:391, Halsey got drunk on a visit to Liberty, Missouri, in 1842, and set out for a fast horseback ride through the woods. A tree branch hit him on the head and he died instantly.

17. Pratte, Chouteau, and Co. became Pierre Chouteau, Jr., and Co. in 1838. The reorganized firm, finding the robe trade a profitable replacement for the greatly reduced beaver trade, expanded its operations on the upper Missouri. Between 1839 and 1842, its capital investment on the upper river rose from $30,000 to $60,000; its trading force increased from 90 to 130 men; and the number of posts grew from fourteen to eighteen. See John E. Sunder, **The Fur Trade on the Upper Missouri, 1840-65** (Norman: University of Oklahoma Press, 1965), p.31.

18. Sunder, p.88.

19. DeSmet was at Fort Union in 1840, 1841, 1851, 1859, 1862, 1863, and 1867.

20. DeSmet, 1:244. Reuben Gold Thwaites, **Early Western Travels, 1748-1846**, vol.27 (being DeSmet's Letters and Sketches, 1841-1842):149.

21. John Francis McDermott, ed., **Up the Missouri With Audubon, The Journal of Edward Harris** (Norman: University of Oklahoma Press, 1951), p.113.

22. Chittenden, **American Fur Trade**, 1:369.

23. Joseph A. Sire, Log Book, 1843, MoHS. Audubon, 2:29.

24. O. A. Stevens, "Audubon's Journey Up the Missouri River, 1843." **North Dakota Historical Society**, 10 (January-October 1943), pp. 74-75. John Francis McDermott, ed., **Audubon in the West**, (Norman: University of Oklahoma Press, 1965), pp. 10 and 10n.

25. Audubon's and Harris's diaries have already been cited. Isaac Sprague's diary is in the Library of the Boston Athenaeum.

26. Audubon, 2:28-29.

27. At Fort Union, Audubon hired Etienne Provost as a guide. Provost had been in the fur country for more than 30 years and was one of the claimants for the discovery of South Pass. McDermott, **Harris**, pp.98 and 98n.

28. Audubon, 2:34-35. McDermott, **Harris**, p. 101. Harris listed the musicians: Culbertson on violin, Denig on Clarinet, and Chardon on drum.

29. Audubon, 2:22, 31, 38, 40-41, 57, 77,108-10, 137, and 182. McDermott, **Audubon**, p. 119. Sprague, "Diary."

30 Audubon, 2:72

31. McDermott, **Harris**, pp. 98, 101, 102, 113, 117, 121, 125,127, 131, 142, 151, and 169.

32. Sprague, "Diary." Issac Sprague, Jr., "Isaac Sprague, 1811-1895." 8 pp.

33. Audubon, 2:180-88.

34. McKenzie, October 8 and 27, 1844, to his wife; and petition for his share in Pierre Chouteau, Jr., and Co., St. Louis, Circuit Court, County of St. Louis, both in McKenzie Papers, MoHS. Perhaps more of this trip would be known had not McKenzie's house burned destroying nearly all his personal papers.

CHAPTER 5

Travelers and Artists

The late 1840s saw an increase in the number of visitors at Fort Union. Mountain man, priest, scientist, and artist found their way to its hospitable table. None other than Jim Bridger, the tallest taleteller in the West, arrived with a group of trappers to spend the winter of 1844-45. Beaver trapping was down to a trickle now; Bridger had already opened his own trading post on the Oregon Trail. But he and his friends would spend this winter in the company of real fur men. William Laidlaw, in charge of the fort that winter, offered Bridger every assistance. However, Laidlaw did not think that Bridger was "a man calculated to manage men, and in my opinion will never succeed in making profitable returns." Indian in habit and deed, these trappers pitched their tipis on the prairie about one-half mile from the fort. There would be plenty of visiting back and forth.[1]

Among the employees at Fort Union at this time was a young Scotsman, Alexander Hunter Murray, who had joined the American Fur Company almost as soon as he came to America. He would work on the upper Missouri from 1844 to 1846 then move to Canada to work for the Hudson's Bay Company. In later years, he was the builder of Fort Yukon in Russia's Alaska and the factor at Lower Fort Garry in Manitoba.

Murray probably would have escaped notice at Fort Union had he not been a talented artist. He sketched the fort as well as several others on the Missouri, including nearby Fort Mortimer. His original sketches have not been found and, since Murray was so painstaking with detail, history is much the poorer. Second-rate copies of his sketches have been preserved; these, with their limitations, provide still another source of information about the fort.[2]

In 1847, the same year the Protestant medical-missionary, Marcus Whitman, was killed in the Oregon Country by the Cayuses, Father Nicholas Point, a Jesuit who had first entered the Pacific Northwest mission field with Father DeSmet, went down the Missouri river for the last time. From Fort Lewis he traveled down to Fort Union by barge; there he caught the steamer **Martha** for St. Louis. While at the post he made two of his small sketches. Like Catlin, Point was better at portraits than at architectural detail. Nevertheless, his sketches also add to the body of knowledge of Fort Union. From St. Louis, Point went to Canada where he died at Quebec City in 1868.[3]

A few months after Point boarded the **Martha**, an adventurer arrived at Fort Union with a new twist. John Palliser, a footloose tourist, decided that he would like to winter at Fort Union. The only other travelers to have done that were Maximilian's party who stayed at Fort Clark during the winter of 1833-34. From Palliser's account we catch a flash of the fort during the long months of cold and quiet.

Old Man Kipp himself was bourgeois of Fort Union that winter and had, in fact, arrived with Palliser on October 27.[4] Kipp, with his many years of experience, was a favorite of the Indians; and two bands came in to welcome him back to the upper river. Palliser spent the shortening fall days hunting buffalo and exploring the wild country.

About Christmas a violent snowstorm brought a temporary stop to hunting and, as Palliser put it, made them prisoners of the fort. To celebrate the holiday, Kipp had a prime, small-boned heifer butchered. The company sat down to Christmas dinner with anticipation. However, one by one, they turned from their heifer steaks to get themselves some real meat—buffalo.

About that time, too, an epidemic swept through the fort. No one knew what it was, except that it was "a sort of cold that affected the throat like mumps." Denig was the acting doctor at the time and did what he could, until he too came down with it. That left

Palliser, alone, responsible for a time to go hunting for meat for the tables.

He recounted that, during the times they were snowbound, they led a very routine sort of life. Bells regulated their day: one to rise by, one for dinner, and one for supper. A cheerful fire brightened the dining room where "our mulatto cook served breakfast, consisting of fried buffalo and venison, round breakfast cakes of wheaten flour . . . and excellent flour, with the luxuries of cream and butter." The noon meal was similar except that there was no coffee with it.

During the winter, some Sioux came into the vicinity of Fort Union. Ordinarily they lived farther down the river where Fort Pierre was the center of their trade. In the future, however, there would be an increasing number of notices concerning Sioux in the vicinity of Fort Union. Their visits were not always welcomed with pleasure. On this occasion they killed several of the fort's milk cows. They also shot the post's purebred bull. In the best tradition, the wounded animal staggered into the fort and died at the foot of the flagstaff. It was a serious blow; the cattle could not be replaced until the next summer.

Palliser went back down to St. Louis in 1848. While in the city he visited Kenneth McKenzie. Undoubtedly he shared his winter's adventures with the ex-bourgeois.[5]

The trade in robes and the company's fortunes held up well in the mid-1840s, despite a few unexpected setbacks. At the end of 1845, Picotte wrote from Fort Pierre that Kipp could "rely that a sufficiency of grog will be brought up" to Fort Union. Meanwhile, Kipp was to promise alcohol so that the Indians would make their hunt.[6] The year 1846, however, was the driest yet on the upper Missouri. The company became embroiled in a serious lawsuit concerning its liquor operations, and Chouteau ordered a temporary stop to smuggling on the Missouri.

Nevertheless, Fort Union succeeded in at least keeping its whistle wet. H. H. Sibley advised the company that in the Red River Settlement there were "several private stills, and where it is probable the article might be procured and transported in carts to some points high up on the Missouri." He recommended as dependable Messrs. McDermot and Sinclair. The next mention of these gentlemen's names was notice that they had been paid $1,774.31 for "skins purchased."[7]

The year 1846 also brought Fort Union its third competitor when

Harvey and Primeau and Company occupied Fort Mortimer, which again was called Fort William.[8] There was not much to compete for at the junction of the rivers two years later. Pierre Chouteau, Jr., wrote in 1848, "The Trade appears to continue as good as ever except at Fort Union where Buff o [sic] disappeared all at once." Edwin Denig, now promoted to bourgeois at Fort Union, felt the effect of this. The bustling scenes that Maximilian had witnessed in 1833 were no more. Where one hundred men had milled about the fort, Denig's staff was down to less than ten by the summer of 1849. The number increased in the wintertime as various small outfits came in from the outposts.[9]

EDWIN THOMPSON DENIG AND MRS. DENIG

Edwin Thompson Denig and Mrs. (Deer Little Woman) Denig, ca 1855. Denig, a long-timer on the Upper Missouri, became bourgeois of Fort Union in the late 1840s. He remained in that position until his retirement in 1856. He, without doubt, was the most intellectual of the traders on the Upper Missouri, having contributed significantly to the ethnology of the Indians of that region. *Courtesy Smithsonian Institution National Anthropological Archives.*

Denig may have been short-handed, but he did not intend to sit around and let the fort fall down upon him. Indeed, under his management, Fort Union reached a new high in elegance. New objects began to appear such as an office water jar and a new clock. Still enjoying his music, Denig also ordered a new "clarinett" and a few reeds for it. He told Culbertson that although he had few men he was going to "put the fort in such a position that the property & people will be secure." If he could find a man who knew how, he would have a lime kiln burned.[10]

In 1850, Alexander Culbertson brought his brother Thaddeus up to Fort Pierre for a visit. Thaddeus, interested in fossils and seeking to improve his health, explored the Badlands then took the steamboat up to Fort Union. He was as impressed by the handsome setting as all those who preceded him. In his journal he recorded only one structural detail that no one else had mentioned—the dimensions of Larpenteur's wicket: "A room also is built against the wall by the gate, in which they used to trade through a small hole about one foot square in the wall."[11]

Thaddeus struck it off well with Denig, who gave him a "very fine bow with a valuable quiver and arrows, which I will keep as a memento of this trip." He did not have much time to enjoy it. He left Fort Union in June and in August died at home, 27 years old, of bilious dysentery.[12]

The next year, 1851, was a landmark of sorts. When Captain Joseph LaBarge tied up the **St. Ange** at Fort Union's landing, the first white woman ever to see the fort was aboard—Mrs. LaBarge. Uncharacteristically, Denig did not make note of this event; we do not know if he entertained Mrs. LaBarge or even if she stepped ashore.[13]

Thoroughly documented is the arrival of Rudolph F. Kurz, a twenty-eight-year-old Swiss who had traveled to America to capture the wild West on canvas. To support himself, he had signed on with the American Fur Company. He had left St. Louis on the same boat as Mrs. LaBarge but had disembarked at Fort Berthold, his first assignment. That September he traveled by horse to Fort Union to report to Denig for work. Approaching the post, Kurz mentioned seeing the "white bastions" from a distance.

Kurz was not overly impressed with his new boss on first meeting him, " a small, hard-featured man wearing a straw hat, the brim of which was turned up in the back." He decided too that Denig was "a rather prosy fellow." However, as soon as Kurz saw the dinner that Denig had had prepared, he changed his mind "at once concerning himself to such a hospitable reception in behalf of a subordinate who was a total stranger to him." Kurz dove into the chocolate, milk, butter, omelet, fresh meat, and hot bread — "What a magnificent spread!"

Kurz's first assignment was to paint the bourgeois's house. Although this was rather far from his kind of painting, he wanted to do a good job because of Denig's kindness to him. "Every evening he sits with me, either in my room or in front of the gate, and relates experiences of his earlier life." Denig told Kurz he had been

This excellent sketch of the bourgeois's house was prepared by the young German artist, Rudolph Friederich Kurz, in 1851. This is the earliest representation of the structure showing the addition of a full second floor, a two-story porch, and a widow's walk. *Courtesy St. Louis University, St. Louis.*

at Fort Union nineteen years (since about 1832). Kurz was especially struck, however, with the fact that Denig had two wives, referred to as the younger one and the older.[14]

In his conversations with Denig, Kurz learned how Pierre Chouteau Jr., and Company had organized the trade on the Missouri and Platte as of 1851:

> Mr. Culbertson is agent for the upper Missouri outfit and has supervision of three posts: Fort Union, Fort Benton, and Fort Alexander. Mr. W. Picotte is agent for the lower Missouri outfit, which includes . . . Fort Pierre, Fort Lookout, Fort Vermilion, Fort Clarke, and Fort Berthold. Mr. Papin is agent on the Platte, having charge of Fort Hall and Fort Laramie. A bourgeois or head clerk is stationed at each post. He receives a fixed salary of $1,000 and a stated percentage on sales.
>
> The less a bourgeois has to pay for the upkeep of fort, in salaries for employees, and for skins and furs the greater will be his profit. . . . Clerks and engagés are paid on an average the wage they receive in the United States, but they are required to buy everything from the trading post. . . .

A craftsman or workman receives $250 a year; a workman's assistant is never paid more than $120; a hunter receives $400, together with the hides and horns of the animals he kills; an interpreter without other employment, which is seldom, gets $500. Clerks and traders who have mastered [Indian languages] . . . may demand from $800 to $1,000 without interest. All employees are furnished board and lodging free of charge.[15]

Kurz quickly learned too that a post had a rigid social organization that could be seen most clearly in the dining room, "Hunters and workmen eat at the second table, i.e., meat, biscuit, and black coffee with sugar." The clerks ate at the bourgeois's table: "We have meat, well selected, bread, frequently soup and pie on Sundays." But everyone, from top to bottom, had to supply his own bedding; "however, one may borrow two buffalo robes from the storeroom."[16]

Kurz described the palisades in much the same manner as others; his remarks showed too that the walls were beginning to show their old age and that repairs were necessary. "The palisades . . . are fitted into heavy beams that rest upon a foundation of limestone." They "are further secured by supports of crossed beams on the inside." While he was at Fort Union, the wall on the west side, "where the supports were badly decayed," blew down before new beams were ready. To Kurz, the job of cutting trees and preparing the timbers for the palisades seemed a most "laborious and difficult task."[17]

Both the north and south gates were still in operation at this time. Kurz told about an Indian on horseback chasing his wife out on the prairie. She reached the fort and banged on the south gate "and before I could let her in . . . the man was already pounding at the opposite gate."

The pressroom that Denig had described in 1843 still served its original purpose. Kurz paid it a visit one day to list all the different kinds of furs in it. He found over twenty species, ranging from mouse to grizzly bear. The ice house also was still in use, "Our only occupation at the moment is the storing of ice in the ice house." He described how some men cut the ice and carry it to the river bank, others load the blocks into a cart, and still others take the cart to the ice house, "and I have to count the number of loads delivered." In mentioning how valuable the ice was in summer, he said that the fort's water supply still came from the river.[18]

On his first night at Fort Union and at a later time, Kurz described the interpreters' room in the western range. It was "rather like an Indian's habitation. On the floor near me were three beds [of buffalo robes] for three couples of half-Indians and their full-blooded wives." On the second occasion, a group of gamblers and on-lookers were in this room, "dimly lighted by the open fire and one candle." The crowd consisted of Indians, whites, and half-breeds; "eight Herantsa and seven Assiniboin sat opposite one another on the floor, encircled about a pile of bows, quivers, knives, calico, etc."

Kurz did not say where his own room was, but it was near enough to the interpreters' that the noise of their gambling kept him awake. On another occasion, he mentioned that his room was near the dining room. Thus it would seem he was in the west end of the main house across the yard from the range containing the interpreters. Except for a leaky roof his room was a comfortable one, "furnished with bedstead, two chairs, and a large table." Later on, he acquired an Indian wife, whose few possessions were added to the scene.[19]

Kurz's painting chores at Fort Union were the subject of many a diary entry. Denig directed him to first paint the front of the bourgeois's house, then to decorate the "reception room" with pictures. Next, he was to paint a life-size portrait of Denig "that is to hang in the office where it will strike the Indians with awe."

The artist gathered his materials from "the principal building, in the warehouse, in garret and cellar." He found "many oil colors (neither very good nor complete)," a marble slab with a grinder, and five measures of oil. Two clerks, Owen McKenzie and Packinaud, came to help him and, on September 6, he began painting the balcony and the reception room. By 1851, the balcony was a two-storied affair, and the central dormer windows upstairs had given away to a full second floor. A gallery, or widow's walk, crowned the top of the house.

Kurz worked very hard on the house and apparently had it finished, as well as the picket fence in front, well before the end of September. Meanwhile, he had other tasks, "Mr. Denig expressed the wish that I paint also a sideboard in the mess hall; it was not sufficiently glary when finished, so he decided to improve its appearance himself." Kurz disliked that kind of painting, so he took care to praise Denig's work highly, "in order to be rid of it once and for all."

Next Kurz undertook portraits of Denig and of Natoh, Denig's favorite dog. The bourgeois gave him permission to do also a watercolor of the bourgeois at Fort William, Joseph Picotte. Although Denig liked only life-sized oil portraits, Kurz undertook to make his boss a copy of a pen and wash sketch he had done of the interior of the fort.[20] In February 1852, Kurz did two more sketches of the interior of the fort from the southwest bastion. All three sketches have survived, all are excellent in their details, and together they tell more about the fort than any number of words.[21]

Kurz spent the winter of 1851-1852 at Fort Union, having been hired as a clerk. The wealth of detail captured here of life within the fort makes Kurz one of the more important artists to have depicted the post. *Courtesy Thomas Gilcrease Institute of American History and Art, Tulsa, Oklahoma.*

The next painting project was to reproduce the likeness of the company's president, Pierre Chouteau, Jr., on the gable above the second-floor porch at the front of the house. Denig gave Kurz a trade medal that had Chouteau's profile on it. Kurz took only two days to do the portrait, but he "had to work in a most uncomfortable position on an unsafe scaffold." Kurz did not mention a painting that many years earlier another clerk, J. B. Moncrevier, had done for the top of the main gate—a treaty of peace between Indians and whites.[22]

One day Denig discovered a nude figure that Kurz had sketched. Denig wanted to hang it in the reception room, but he was so unwise as to make some crude jokes about it. Kurz became angry. He probably refused to let go of this particular picture; he wrote later that "for the sake of keeping on good terms with my bourgeois I began to paint another female figure, but not entirely in the nude."[23]

On his next visit to the fort, Alexander Culbertson was so impressed with the oil of Denig that he wanted one of himself. Kurz was troubled by the lack of proper materials, "ceruse, black, vermilion, Prussian blue, yellow ochre, and chrome yellow are the only colors I have, while my brushes are those used, in general, for the beard and for flat painting." He finished the portrait however, and it was hung in the reception room where Indian women and children soon damaged it.[24]

Still other assignments came Kurz's way. He had to paint the bourgeois's three-dog sleigh (a cariole) red and black. About this time Denig hit upon the idea of Kurz's undertaking the painting of fifteen-foot flags, each having an eagle in the center on stripes of red and white. Denig would use these as gifts for Indian leaders or would trade them for "the handsome price of 20 robes apiece." One of these eagle flags joined the portrait in Denig's office. Kurz attended a meeting in this office between Denig and Le Tout Pique, a Cree chief. His busy pen sketched this scene, including the flag and the oil.[25]

Ever since the first cannon arrived at Fort Union, it was the practice to fire a salute for every arriving and departing boat and distinguished visitor. On January 2, 1852, Kurz acquired the job of firing a three-gun salute for a band of Absarokas approaching the fort. It was not an easy task:

> I fired three times with our 4-pounder that stands on the gallery above the river gate. As there were neither cartridges nor match cord at the fort I had to wrap a load of powder in paper and thrust it into the barrel, then ram it with shreds and rags of leather, clear out the vent with an iron pin, put powder on the pan and touch it off with a burning brand. And all by myself. It was in loading the gun after this clumsy fashion that old Gareau . . . lost an arm. He thought it unnecessary, after having fired, to stop the vent while reloading.[26]

The painting projects out of the way, Kurz was appointed to the more responsible position of clerk. His duties included opening the gates every morning, closing them in the evenings, opening them during the night if visitors came, reporting all strangers found outside the fort, keeping an eye on the two bastions and their contents, managing of the press room, supervising the meat supply, assisting at saddling and unsaddling horses, and looking after the tools.

It was this last assignment that vexed Kurz. He found tools everywhere—in the saddle room, meat house, storeroom, outhouses, bastions, even thrust under beds. What was so aggravating to him was Denig's expectation that Kurz know where everything was at any given moment. In a fit of temper, Kurz wrote, "Mr. Denig would be supremely happy to be put in command of at least 10,000 men. . . . To command is his greatest pleasure; desire to command his most characteristic trait."

Part of the problem was that Kurz received his position as clerk at the same time Denig and Culbertson were sitting down to some serious drinking, as was the wont of just about everyone in the fur industry except Charles Larpenteur. Kurz recalled that neither man was sober enough to give him instructions, and that someone gave him "a bunch of ten keys" with no instructions as to what they were for. Still, Kurz had to admit that he had learned a lot lately, including the differences between tallow and lard, between tender and tough meat, and between ox steaks and cow steaks. "It is quite a while," he wrote, "before one knows all the various terms for fresh meat, cured meat, lard, corn, water, 'open the door,' etc., in seven different languages." Denig might get cross when the young clerk forgot to feed the pigeons or failed to praise the younger Mrs. Denig's new ball gown; yet there were more days when Kurz liked Denig than there were days he did not.[27]

There were times for fun too, such as the dance the engagés gave, at their own expense, in the dining room. Or the ball that Denig gave to which he invited all the men and their families from the opposition fort. "We decorated the room as brilliantly as we could with mirrors, candles, precious fur skins, and Indian ornaments," described Kurz. As for Denig, he had to play the fiddle all night, there being no one else who knew how. Kurz, since he did not dance, "beat the tattoo on the drum" and played a tambourine. Fort William returned the favor within the week, which ball was the occasion for another excellent sketch of Fort Union by Kurz.

Then there was the day of the Indian attack. One evening, a horse guard, Joe Delores, galloped up to the gate screaming, "Blackfeet!"

Everyone poured out to help get the horse herd into the fort before the Blackfeet stole them. The rumor flashed that the Blackfeet were in the Garden Coulee, east of the fort. "With great trouble," reported Kurz, "the men got all the horses together just as a man emerged from the spot where the enemy was suspected. Who should it be but our negro, Auguste! He had been looking for berries."[28]

There were, however, Indians at Fort Union that winter. Back in November, Kurz had written that there were so many Indians around that Denig was planning to have an Indian lodge built. As it was, the visitors were crowded "into at least five rooms already occupied." An Indian village of thirty tipis stood on the south bank of the Missouri. Kurz thought the view was most romantic with the tipis in relief against the forest, the bare trees laden with snow. At the same time, on the north bank, set on the gleaming snow-covered prairie stood:

> a group of gaily colored tents with their attendant poles from which are suspended trophies, such as scalps, buffalo beards, strips of red cloth, etc. . . . men walking about . . . youths at their games, girls carrying water, women trudging in with wood, cleaning and scraping hides; horses grazing or near their owners' tents . . . a multitude of dogs.[29]

Besides the various structural details of the post itself, Kurz's diary mentions various places and activities outside the fort with which earlier visitors had become acquainted. Like Audubon, he climbed hills to the north in order to enjoy the view of the Yellowstone and beyond. He dropped down the east side of the hills into the upper part of Garden Coulee. "I was forcing my way through . . . (the deep bed of a dried-up stream thickly overgrown with coppices and bushes, over against which lies our potato garden)." He jumped "across the now insignificant brook and was proceeding with rapid strides toward the horse pasture when I heard a rustling of dry leaves behind me and someone laughed." Fortunately, the noise came from two friendly Assiniboins.

When Kurz was at Fort Union, the timber yard apparently was up the river a short distance. In October, when some Indians left, he wrote, "They were to be put across the river near the timber yard because that's the place where the boats are kept." On another occasion, he noted that someone had gone to "the 'Chantier,' a place in the forest up the river where workmen and laborers . . . are getting beams ready for the palisades." In his third mention of the timber yard he said simply, "workmen set out for the timber yard to get lumber ready to build the new Indian lodge at the fort."[30]

Maximilian commented on the new powder magazine in the fall of 1833 but did not mention its location. Kurz described it as being to the rear of the warehouse. While such a description could mean to the north or to the east, archeological excavations indicate that it was at the north end of the store range.[31]

Kurz's stay at Fort Union lasted only seven months. In the spring of 1852, he got ready to go down the river, taking his precious sketches home to Switzerland. Did he later think back much on his days at Fort Union? Did he ever recall the cold winter day when there was no firewood except in Denig's quarters? Kurz's diary told of the bourgeois sitting there "quite comfortable in his large arm-chair, smoking his short-stem pipe beside his iron stove that glows with a rousing fire. The instant I . . . hold my hands over the delectable base burner . . . the bourgeois invariably finds a new task that takes me into the cold." And did he ever think again of his fellow workers, the French Canadians? He did not like them at Fort Union because they boasted too much about their homeland. He recorded the derisive little song

> Je suis de Canada
> Je me font de ca
> J'ai des pommes de terre
> Pour passer l'hiverre.
>
> (I am from Canada
> I am a part of it
> I have potatoes
> Enough to pass the winter.)[32]

But the time had come to go. On April 18, Kurz wrote, "Fare thee well, Fort Union! Mr. Culbertson arrived by boat yesterday. He will take Morgan and me."[33] Another actor passed from Fort Union's stage.

Notes

1. Larpenteur, **Forty Years**, 2:211. Laidlaw, December 18, 1844, to P. Chouteau, Jr., & Co., Folder 1844, Chouteau Coll., MoHS.

2. **Forest and Stream** (1908), pp.49 and 212. Alexander Hunter Murray, **Journal of the Yukon, 1847-48**, ed. by L. J. Burpee, Publications of the Canadian Archives, No. 4 (Ottawa, 1910), pp. 1-5.

3. Nicholas Point, **Wilderness Kingdom, Indian Life in the Rocky Mountains, 1840-1847**, trans. Joseph P. Donnelly (New York: Holt, Rinehart and Winston, 1967), p.8.

4. At this time, Honoré Picotte was in charge of the Upper Missouri Outfit. He had his headquarters at the larger Fort Pierre rather than at the better built Fort Union.

5. John Palliser, **The Solitary Hunter, or, Sporting Adventures in the Prairies** (London, 1856), pp.79-99, 149, and 207-210.

6. Picotte, December 18, 1846, to Kipp, Fort Pierre Letter Book, Chouteau Coll., MoHS.

7. H. H. Sibley, February 23 and July 6, 1846, to P. Chouteau, Jr., and Co., Folder 1846, Chouteau Coll., MoHS.

8. Sunder, pp.87-95. This was Alexander Harvey who had shot and killed a man in the retail store at Fort Union in 1840. Harvey was one of those who were active in getting the liquor suits pressed against Chouteau.

9. Letter, unsigned and undated, Fort Pierre Letter Book, 1849-50, Folder 1849, Chouteau Coll., MoHS. The initials "AC" are on the letter, possibly indicating Alexander Culbertson.

10. Denig, December 1, 1849, to Culbertson, Folder 1849, Chouteau Coll., MoHS.

11 Thaddeus A. Culbertson, **Journal of an Expedition to the Mauvaises Terres and the Upper Missouri in 1850**, ed. John Francis McDermott, Bureau of American Ethnology Bulletin 147, Smithsonian Institution (Washington, 1952), p.105.

12 **Ibid.**, pp.2 and 12-13.

13. Sunder, p.138.

14. Rudolph Friederich Kurz, **Journal of Rudolph Friederich Kurz**, trans. Myrtis Jarrell, ed. J. N. B. Hewitt, Bureau of American Ethnology Bulletin 115, Smithsonian Institution (Washington, 1937), pp.120, 122, 126, and 210. Edwin Thompson Denig, **Five Indian Tribes of the Upper Missouri**, ed. John C. Ewers (Norman: University of Oklahoma Press, 1961), pp. xxiv-xxv. In 1847, Father Point had reproached Denig for having two wives. Denig reacted by putting a stop to the priest's hitherto unfettered efforts to instill his moral code. In 1856, however, Denig formally married his younger wife, and she accompanied him to Canada upon retirement in 1858.

15. Kurz, pp.234-36.

16. **Ibid.**, p.236.

17. **Ibid.**, pp.122n and 124.

18. **Ibid.**, pp.224, 239, 302, and 329.

19. **Ibid.**, pp.120-21, 137, 200, and 243.

20. This sketch, dated September 19, 1851, was located in a collection of Nicholas Point's sketches at St. Louis University.

21. Kurz, pp.121-22, 127-30, 133, 137, 141, and 292.

22. **Ibid.**, pp.156 and 159. Audubon, 2:185.

23. Kurz, pp.166-67.

24. **Ibid.**, p.223-24.

25. **Ibid.**, pp.134, 243, and 247-48. John C. Ewers, **Artists of the Old West** (New York: Doubleday, 1965), p.144.

26. Kurz, p.256.

27. **Ibid.**, pp.223, 226, and 240-41.

28. **Ibid.**, pp.121,124, and 126

29. **Ibid.**, pp.226 and 244.

30. **Ibid.**, pp.122, 124, 159, 201, 293, and 305.

31. **Ibid.**, p.202.

32. **Ibid.**, pp.110, 123, and 229.

33. **Ibid.**, p. 329.

CHAPTER 6

Sioux and Soldiers

As Fort Union approached its 25th birthday, there were signs of coming change on the upper Missouri. There were still immense herds of buffalo, but white men's civilization was beginning to encroach on the homelands of the plains Indians. In 1853 Fort Union played host to a group of explorers surveying for a railroad route.

The arrival of Isaac I. Stevens's party almost rivaled in show the parades of the Assiniboins in former days:

> During the march in, the governor took his horse, the first time in several days, and rode at the head of the Column. An American flag, made on the way, to the manufacture of which I contributed a red flannel, was carried in the foreward rank, and flags, with appropriate devices, representing the parties carrying them, were respectively carried by the various corps. The Engineer party, a long locomotive running down a buffalo, with the motto 'Westward Ho!' Our meterological party—the Rocky Mountain, with a barometer mounted ... with inscription 'Excelsior.' The astronomical party had a device representing the azure field dotted with stars, the half-moon and a telescope. . . . Teamsters, packmen, hunters, and etc., also carried their insignia.

71

Assiniboin Encampment on the Upper Missouri by John Mix Stanley, who visited **Fort Union in 1853.** *Courtesy Founders Society Detroit Institute of Arts.*

Stevens's description of the fort was a hurried one and does not deserve very much emphasis. For example, he described the bastions as being at the northwest and southeast corners of the fort, the north side as being the front, and the size as being "probably 250 feet square." Of more interest is Stevens's impression of Alexander Culbertson, "a man of great energy, intelligence, and fidelity, and possesses the entire confidence of the Indians." Mrs. Culbertson, "a full-blood Indian of the Blood band of the Blackfoot tribe, is also held in high estimation. Though she appears to have made little or no progress in our language, she has acquired the manners . . . of the white race with singular facility."[1]

With Stevens was John Mix Stanley, the principal artist of the expedition. Not only did Stanley sketch the fort and the Assiniboins receiving their annuities, he made the first daguerreotypes of the fort and area. Stevens noted that "the Indians were greatly pleased with their daguerreotypes." Unfortunately, these pictures are not known to exist today. They possibly were destroyed in the 1865 Smithsonian fire that consumed over 200 of Stanley's western paintings.[2]

Another group of Army explorers arrived at Fort Union in 1856 aboard the **St. Mary.** Along with Lt. G. K. Warren and his seven-

teen enlisted men of the 2d Infantry was F. V. Hayden, who later
would become famous for his western explorations. Warren did not
have very much to do while at Union; he did set up a sixteen-inch
transit and took observations "during a whole lunation; but owing to the cloudy condition of the nights during the time, and the
shortness of the nights themselves, only two sets of observations
were obtained on the moon and stars." He did record the longitude

In 1853, Governor Isaac I. Stevens led a railroad survey party past Fort Union.
John Mix Stanley, the official artist, prepared this drawing of Assiniboins receiving their annuities outside the fort. To the right, a new tower bearing a flag
appears. *Courtesy Fort Union Trading Post NHS.*

of the fort as being 104°02′, with a limit of error of about 10′. This
measurement is of interest for, nearly 100 years later, there was
still confusion as to whether the fort site was in North Dakota or
Montana.[3] Hayden made estimates as to the size of the various
bands of Assiniboins. The results of the smallpox were still evident; his estimation of the entire population came to a little over
2,000.[4]

Hayden did not mention if he met Indian Agent Edwin A. C.
Hatch, who was waiting at Fort Union for the **St. Mary** to take
him up river. Hatch, who appears to have been utterly bored with
his job, did mention one or two incidents of that summer. About
a month before the boat arrived, two men went out to hunt for
stolen horses, "Mr. Chambers returned clothed in a silk
handkerchief-- Shucette in pants and shirt--they were surprised by

73

a war party and Shucette lost my horse and Chambers the one he rode."

Later, Hatch met Jim Bridger, "the old guide and mountain trapper" himself. Bridger was on the upper river that year with Sir George Gore, who was a few days behind at this time. Hatch had an opportunity to visit with Bridger (who apparently stopped at Fort William rather than at Union) and "was much amused with some of his tales of mountain life." Sir George finally arrived at Fort Union and prepared to sail down the Missouri. He had spent the winter of 1855-56 slaughtering huge numbers of wildlife under Bridger's guidance. Failing now to get a satisfactory price for his wagons and carts from Culbertson, Gore had them piled up in front of the fort and set on fire.[5]

This was the same summer that Edwin Denig decided to retire. He was still a relatively young man, but he had been on the upper Missouri almost a quarter of a century. He, Culbertson, Larpenteur, and a few others were among the last of those who had memories of the early Upper Missouri Outfit. Besides running the fort, discussing art and religion with men like Kurz, and writing detailed descriptions of the fort for Audubon, Denig had spent considerable time compiling all he knew about the Indian tribes of the upper Missouri. These documents later came to have a very great importance to ethnologists, among whom Denig may be ranked with the best.

Another contribution of Denig's was his painstaking efforts to assist scientists to collect and prepare specimens for study. The Smithsonian Institution in Washington, DC, received during these years a considerable number of skins and skulls of the mammals and birds found on the upper Missouri that Denig had prepared.

Now it was time to say goodbye to old friends like Culbertson. John Ewers suspects it was Culbertson who, on a visit to his Pennsylvania home in 1832, had persuaded his neighbor, Denig, to join the American Fur Company. Denig himself had almost no family to return to; he and his Indian wife moved to Canada.[6]

Denig picked a good year to leave. A few months later, in January 1857, his replacement, James Kipp, again, wrote to St. Louis to describe the renewed horror of a smallpox epidemic. The opposition's steamboat had brought the pox up to Fort William, "instead of putting their sick ashore" farther down. The disease had begun to spread among the Assiniboins in November; "the loss up to time of writing is estimated at 300 souls." Also, the Crows, who had escaped the 1837 epidemic, were suffering greatly. The Indians scattered far and wide in an effort to escape. The result would be, thought Kipp, a reduction in trade by about one half.

In addition to the smallpox, another trouble had arrived in the form of 400 Sioux. On December 1, 1856, they "stole all our horses, wounded one of our people . . . killed an Assiniboine back of the fort;—they also killed a free white man, trapping on the Yellow Stone, about 8 miles from this place."[7]

As troublesome as the Sioux were becoming, there was from time to time more violence among the employees themselves. Larpenteur described the three-day Christmas party of 1858 when he, as usual, was the sober bartender:

> At the height of the spree the tailor and one of the carpenters had a fight in the shop, while others took theirs outside, and toward evening I was informed that Marseillais, our hunter, had been killed and thrown into the fireplace. We immediately ran in, and, sure enough, there he was, badly burned and senseless, but not dead yet.

The bourgeois had the tailor and a carpenter arrested and placed in irons. Later, they received a "trial by jury," were found guilty, and administered thirty-nine lashes each.[8]

Charles (Carl) Wimar's dramatic 1859 painting of *Indians Approaching Fort Union*. This magnificent painting shows the opposition post, Fort William, to the left, the confluence of the Yellowstone and Missouri rivers, the Assiniboins, and Fort Union to the right. No other 19th century artist captured the essence of the Upper Missouri fur trade as did Wimar. *Courtesy Washington University Gallery of Art, St. Louis.*

Carl (Charles) Wimar, a German immigrant living in St. Louis, came up the river in 1858, but too early for the Christmas party. He published an account of his journey in a German newspaper;

however, it did not describe the fort in any detail. More importantly, Wimar was a very good artist, and he sketched six of the company's Missouri river forts, including Union. The original sketches have not been found; fortunately they were printed in Chittenden's work on Pierre DeSmet. At Fort Union, Wimar climbed the bluffs north of the fort and from there did the preliminary work for a grand panoramic oil painting of the confluence of the Missouri and Yellowstone, including both Forts Union and William and a band of Assiniboins approaching.[9] Still another artist followed Wimar to Fort Union, in 1860. This was William Jacob Hays of New York

In 1860, William J. Hays of New York visited Fort Union. Later, he completed this fine oil. The robe press is shown in some detail. Deterioration seems to be setting in on the rockwork of the bastion, whereon the third-floor room has been added. *Courtesy Glenbow Foundation, Calgary, Canada.*

who traveled on the **Spread Eagle** that summer. Like Wimar, he left no written descriptions of importance, but he did execute at least one sketch and one very fine oil of the fort.[10]

The Army made a brief appearance at Fort Union in the summer of 1860 when Captain William F. Raynolds and First Lieutenant Henry E. Maynadier of the Yellowstone Expedition camped for two weeks near the junction of the two rivers. The troops called their site Camp Humphreys, "in honor of the distinguished officer in charge of the Bureau of Explorations and Surveys."

The officers visited Bourgeois Robert Meldrum at the fort and purchased such supplies as flour, sugar, and coffee. Since they were to go down the river on boats, Raynolds sold his forty horses to

Fort Union at $5 each. Lieutenant Maynadier was surprised at the good order of life at the fort, especially on the evening of August 4 when he attended a ball: "Although the ladies were the daughters of the forest, they were attired in the fashionable style of the States, with hoops and crinoline." The troops left on August 15, "As soon as the bow of the boat swung round the flag was unfurled, which was the signal for a salute. The flag on the fort was run up and guns fired as long as we were in sight."[11]

The number of boats on the upper Missouri increased considerably as the United States became more deeply involved with the Civil War. A number of citizens of Missouri with Confederate sympathies, or, perhaps more correctly, who did not have strong Union sympathies, undertook to migrate to the Pacific Slope. The discovery of gold in Idaho and western Montana gave further stimulus to travel. Besides the Oregon Trail, travelers could reach the Pacific Northwest with increasing ease by taking a steamboat all the way to Fort Benton then continuing on Mullan's Road to their destination. For these travelers, Fort Union became but a way stop. Still, it was an impressive place; and a number of descriptions appeared in the journals and letters of the time.

One such visitor in 1861 was John Mason Brown who traveled up river on the **Spread Eagle**. As they slipped by Fort William, the passengers noted that it had finally been abandoned; the last of the opposition had given up. Then came Fort Union: "Salutes passed between boat and Fort. No Indians in the neighborhood who should be here to receive annuities, viz Crows & Assiniboins. Sioux lurking about."

Brown met the bourgeois, Robert Meldrum, whom he thought to be a pleasant man. Meldrum showed Brown his "snow machine," but Brown did not explain what it was. He did not think much of the fort's defenses, "The two bastions utterly unfit for the 4 pounders which they contain." He misjudged the size of the fort considerably (100 x 200 yards) but allowed it was well arranged. He was very much "Amused at a tame Grizzly Bear kept at the Fort who diverted himself by boxing the pigs and frightening the horses of a few Assinaboins who came in last evening."

The fur trade interested him somewhat, and Brown found that "the trade of this post has been steadily declining for some years, the Indians finding it more convenient to traffic higher up the river." The **Chippewa**, a shallow-draft steamboat, arrived to take

77

passengers and supplies up the river; the **Spread Eagle** took on 24,000 robes "principally from Fort Benton brought down in Mackinac boats" and left for St. Louis.[12]

Another visitor who saw the "pet" grizzly in 1861, before she got away, was William H. Schieffelin. He and two companions, William M. Cary and an Emlen N. Lawrence, all from New York City, were on a travel adventure that eventually took them to the Pacific coast then home by way of Panama. Cary sketched the sights they saw, while Schieffelin wrote of their experiences. They had meant to remain at Fort Union only long enough for the **Chippewa** to load. They left on schedule, but the **Chippewa** exploded and sank, destroying eighty of Cary's sketches. The adventurers returned to Fort Union for another six weeks waiting for other means to continue their trip.

A trio of adventurers from New York City visited Fort Union in 1861. One of them, William Cary, served as artist of their exploits. Although many of his sketches were destroyed when his steamboat blew up, this engraving is extant. Apparently it is a "negative" illustration because only with a reverse printing can sense be made of the scene. The illustration shows the back gate; therefore, the bastion should be on the left (east). Nevertheless, this is the only known drawing depicting a Sioux raid on Fort Union. *Courtesy Frank Leslie's Illustrated Newspaper, May 30, 1868.*

They spent the six weeks hunting, riding, and becoming acquainted with Indians. At one time a large band of Assiniboins came in and camped. The whites witnessed the Indian dances and horse races. The troublesome Sioux were still in the area. On one occasion, a party of haymakers came across three wounded white trappers, only a few miles from the fort. At another time, unidentified Indians successfully stole six horses from the fort's herd.

Before leaving, the young men invested $10 in a party for the entire fort staff. "The orchestra consisted of one old fiddle and a fife, played by several volunteers. . . . The old trappers and their squaws seemed to enjoy the dancing more than [the visitors] . . . there was no round dancing, or German." Schieffelin described the scene, "The dancers all wore solemn faces, and worked as if earning wages. They jumped, stamped, slapped their thighs and clapped their hands. . . . In fact, the dance was a sort of mixture of negro breakdown and Irish jig." The sponsors were told that the party was a complete success, "inasmuch as it ended in a fight and a stabbing affray."[13]

Later that year, the Sioux approached Fort Union with aggression in mind. This time about 250 of them "killed 25 head of cattle, burnt all the out houses & 280 Tons of Hay and two Mac Kinaw Boats." According to the report, they attempted to set fire to the fort itself, but left when one of them was killed and two others wounded. The damage would have been more extensive had not sixty-five cattle and twenty-seven horses been dispatched to Fort Benton just two days earlier.[14]

James Harkness, a member of the firm of LaBarge, Harkness & Co., stopped at Fort Union in June 1862. He reported that the past winter had been extremely cold and that the Indians had suffered a loss of 500 horses because of the storms. It was his opinion that the "fort is on a good site, but fast going to decay." He too noted the increasing menace of the Sioux, saying that the fort personnel no longer went outside the walls without being fully armed.[15]

Henry A. Boller, who had been at Fort Union in 1858, returned for a visit in 1863. In contrast to John Mason Brown, Boller thought the fort was very strong. "The bastions were of stone, and the massive and substantial pickets were braced and secured in the strongest manner." He referred to the bourgeois's house as an "ornamental" building, and recalled with pleasure that "around its hospitable board and on its balcony, during the pleasant summer evenings, was gathered a social circle." His own quarters were in one of the bastions, "which commanded a most extensive and delightful view." This was the first notice of a guest being put up in the bastion. Sometime between 1853 and 1858, the roof of the southwest bastion had been raised and a wooden-walled room, in effect a third story, added. Perhaps this was the room given Boller.

He commented on the state of trade, confirming the opinions of other recent travelers, "Fort Union, in 1863, was (and had been for several years past) simply a Post for the Assiniboin Indians, and as they are notoriously poor robe-makers, its trade had fallen away very considerably." Then, too, there were the Sioux, who staged a raid while Boller was present.

One September morning he was in the bastion cleaning his weapons and resting. Suddenly, he realized that some half-breed children, who had been playing outside, were all crying. "In a half-hesitating manner I stepped out upon the gallery. What a sight met my gaze! The whole sandbar seemed literally alive with naked savages, who . . . were making directly for the Fort!"

The cook and his Indian wife had gone down to the river to get kettles of water. The Sioux chased the poor couple, but they apparently escaped when Boller fired into the leading warriors, wounding two. Also endangered were the wood-choppers and a few men who had gone upstream to hunt and fish. All managed to get back to the fort safely. It was not really an attack but a very good scare. Raids of this type had become so frequent, Boller noted, that Fort Union no longer bothered to keep milk cows and had abandoned the garden completely. The time was close when a few soldiers would be most welcome.[16]

Major General John Pope, in 1863, directed campaigns against the Sioux farther downstream, in retaliation for their violent attacks on Minnesota settlements in 1862. Although meeting with some success, Pope decided that he would have to mount new campaigns in 1864. Part of his plan was to establish additional army forts along the Missouri. Indian Agent Samuel Lotta thought this an excellent idea. He recommended Fort Union as an ideal place for a military post. From there, the troops could keep a watch on British traders and on any Southern sympathizers that might be at Union, as well as protect the area from the Sioux.[17]

Brigadier General Alfred Sully led between two and three thousand men across the Little Missouri badlands toward the Yellowstone river in the summer of 1864. His intentions were to defeat any Sioux encountered, then to build a permanent post on the Yellowstone. Meanwhile, supplies came up the Missouri by boat and were stored at Fort Union.

The overland march was exhausting; dysentery appeared in the command. By the time the troops reached the Yellowstone on August 12, they were worn, hungry, and dispirited. Two steamers were waiting for them, which raised morale greatly. Sully decided not to build a fort that season but to move down the Yellowstone to its mouth and then continue home.[18]

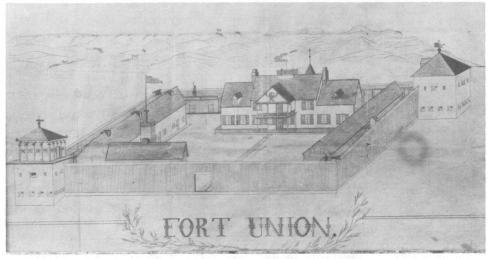

This handsome pen-and-ink, hand-tinted drawing of Fort Union is believed to have been done by Benjamin Franklin Griffin, a soldier in Company I, 30th Wisconsin Infantry Regiment, which was stationed at the fort 1864-1865. *Courtesy Fort Union Trading Post NHS.*

Company I, 30th Wisconsin Infantry, had arrived at Fort Union in June to guard the military supplies until Sully arrived. When Sully did appear, he was not at all impressed with Fort Union as a potential site for a permanent army post. To him, it was too far run down and not at the best location. At the junction of the rivers, on the sites of old Forts William and Mortimer, he picked out an area that he thought would be more suitable on which to build. It was here that the Army built Fort Buford two years later.[19]

At least two men in Sully's command recorded their impressions of Fort Union. Amos R. Cherry, Company B, 14th Iowa Infantry, wrote on August 18, "Crossed [Missouri] River. Arms and Equipment carried over in 'Yawl.' Horses swim across river. All pass safely. Fort Union is very pretty place indeed nice painted in fine style." Two days later a volunteer named Overholt took a look around Fort Union, "it is an old French fort and was built for an Indian mission in eighteen thirty." However, Overholt did not give an opinion as to whether he thought it dilapidated as did his general, or pretty as did Cherry.[20]

Sully's command moved on down the Missouri, while Company I remained behind to guard the supplies that had been meant for the fort that was not built. Thirty years earlier, Charles Larpenteur had kept a detailed diary during a very active period at Fort Union; now he was back and again he would log the daily events for the next year—a year in which fur trader and soldier tried to live side by side. Larpenteur was a clerk on that earlier occasion, and now he was bourgeois; however, Fort Union was not quite the establishment it had been in McKenzie's day. When Larpenteur arrived at Union early in the morning of May 31, 1864, he found "not a Single horse nor ox team to haul up the freight and but very few men about the Fort," and most of them drunk. He was driven to getting women to help him.

June started off in a grand order. The Assiniboins arrived on June 4 for trade and, like in the old days, "very fine dances given in the fort to the whites." Meanwhile, the Indians camped below the garden ravine, where Larpenteur was able to gather some asparagus. Indian Agent Mahlon Wilkinson issued the annual annuities at a council on June 11.

Then, on June 13, the **Yellow Stone** arrived and Larpenteur described the sudden blossoming of "two fine rows of tents . . . in the Center of the Fort." Company I, 30th Wisconsin Infantry, had arrived. The government's and the company's supplies were stored in the supply rooms, and Larpenteur sat back to watch the troops, more of whom arrived on the **Well Come** on July 17. Two days later, the traders witnessed "a dress parade and inspection." Larpenteur thought "the drill was very well preformed and the Indians were quite pleased."

Twenty-nine years earlier, Larpenteur had witnessed the construction of the storerooms. Now, in the afternoon of June 30, "a great crash was heard in the Stores." When he investigated, he discovered "that the principal Beam which supported the Joists had given away which occasioned all the Joists to break off in the middle." However, except for boxes of soap and candles, the damage was not as bad as it had first seemed. Within a few days the broken joists were removed and props were placed under the main beam.

Over the years, July 4 had often passed unobserved at Fort Union. In the heyday of the fur trade, the fort's personnel were usually too busy to take more than note of the holiday. The Army's policy was somewhat different. On the morning of July 4, Larpenteur was awakened "very early by the firing of Six Cannons which broke several pains [sic] of glass in the Fort." That was but the beginning. After dark that evening, the "Captain had two Shells fired"; these were followed by "fire balls." As late as July 7, the sober bourgeois noted that there was still considerable drinking going on.

Despite the presence of the soldiers, Larpenteur tried to arrange his business as it had always been done at the post. He directed his men (sometimes helped by soldiers) to clean out the interior of the post, had some haul wood, and had others prepare and fire charcoal pits, and he took an inventory of supplies. During the inventory, he discovered "that Something like fifty vials of Strychnac had been stolen out of the Medisene cupboard."

On July 14, he noted that the second (of about four) editions of the **Frontier Scout** was published by Robert Winegar and Ira F. Goodwin of Company I. Larpenteur regretted there was not more news at Fort Union to encourage them to publish more often.[21]

A band of 25 Sioux upset the equilibrium of the post at dawn, July 23. They rushed the horse guard and captured all 17 horses, "passing them within one hundred yards of the Fort." Two detachments of soldiers gave chase later but they accomplished nothing. At least it would make some news for the paper.

Larpenteur had noted that the river was changing its course—closer toward the fort, he hoped. But on July 25, when there were no fewer than five steamboats at Union--**Bell Peoria, Chippewa Falls, Alone, General Grant,** and **Benton**--the men were "obliged to make half loads [of the cargoes] in order to cross over the bar in front of the Fort."

Three weeks later, he noted the arrival of Sully's army, surely the largest number of men to pass by Fort Union in many a year. It was Larpenteur's opinion that Sully had "done but little or nothing with the Sioux." On the other hand, he learned that nine men drowned trying to cross the Yellowstone, and one more lost his life crossing the Missouri to Fort Union. Soon, the troops were gone and "none but Company I and the Fort Union men on hand."

Larpenteur made note of the several construction projects undertaken by the troops. They erected their own store rooms "next to the pickets," set up a sawmill, built "another root house or an underground Store room," and made hay. At the same time, Larpenteur's own men made hay, built a roof for the hay mow, and put a new covering of earth on the stables. On September 7, he "employed the Carpenter at making a flight of Stairs to go up to the uper [sic] Story [of the bourgeois house] without going in to

This photograph of Fort Union shows the bourgeois's house in 1866. A staircase leads to the second floor where Charles Larpenteur had his quarters. The U.S. Army had occupied the ground floor. *Illingworth and Bill Photograph, Courtesy Montana Historical Society, Helena.*

the main entrense [sic]." These steps appeared in the only known photograph of the house, taken two years later.

Around the middle of September, the Crows came in and a second annuity council was held. Larpenteur then commenced trading. He procured enough robes so that the Army cleared its supplies out of the company's warehouse for storing the robes. About this time, the blacksmith left the post, "not being willing to do as he was required to do."

As the cooler days of autumn approached, the soldiers turned to building themselves winter quarters. They rafted logs down the river, worked hard at putting up the buildings, and had their houses finished by October 1, except for the bunks. They then turned to the construction of wooden quarters for the officers, a blacksmith shop, and an ice house and to the weatherboarding of their "flour and stuff stored under the Fort gallery."

Larpenteur's own men undertook a multitude of tasks at this time: hauling firewood, drawing coals, building a trough to "turn the rain from the Store roof off of the hay," weatherboarding the stores, moving the cooking utensils from the kitchen building to the dining room for the winter, rendering grease, repairing the window blinds on the bourgeois's house, daubing the old kitchen, repairing its roof, and whitewashing it. The carpenter went over the main house making repairs, and the tops of the paling fence in front were painted.

Still other jobs involved whitewashing the outside of the men's quarters, hauling seven logs for repairing the ice house, enlarging "the space of the counter" (in the retail store?), constructing a pig pen, daubing the blacksmith shop and the ice house, whitewashing the latter, and butchering a hog. The soldiers kept pace by rebuilding the gallery around the fort so that they could walk from one bastion to the other on their guard mounts. They also prepared a room to be used as a hospital.

On November 22, a group of miners arrived from Montana on their way back to the States. Larpenteur wrote that they were "a poor looking sett of broken down gold seakers   we cannot give them much room." These miners called themselves the Idaho Company and were a great trial to Larpenteur over the winter. In March, he got construction started on a boat for them and, on April 17, was able to say, "Great and Glorious, the Idao Company have started at last under a salute of two of shots of the largest guns of Fort Union . . . their boat went full sail." Immediately, he had his men clean out the rooms the miners had rented.

Before leaving the winter of 1864-65, notice must be made of the troops. On February 4, Larpenteur noted that scurvy had appeared among the soldiers. During a warm spell, he observed that those sick from scurvy were brought out to sun. Then, on March 17, "One of the soldiers died at half past 10 oclock last night it is said of the scurvy." He made a similar entry on April 4, April 6, April 24, and May 7.

By April 1865, however, spring was on its way. All the stoves came down on the 19th. The kitchen was whitewashed and the cook moved back to it. However, he took sick about this time and, nine days later, died.

On April 27, three soldiers went down to the point below the fort to hunt. About twenty-five Sioux attacked them. One soldier "was shot through and killed on the spot but all with arrows   he had eleven wounds all with arrows and was scalped and entirely strip of his clothing." One of his companions was severely wounded, but the surgeon thought he might recover. The third man was not hit and he managed to kill one Sioux. After they had buried their dead companion the next day, the soldiers went out and hanged the body of the dead Sioux.

Whether or not it was the fever of spring, Larpenteur spent May 1865 having the fort spruced up. The "big house" got all its doors and chair boards painted. The carpenter constructed a "plank way" from the kitchen to the main house to overcome the eternal mud. For several days the men whitewashed and painted here and there.

FORT UNION, WASHINGTON TERRITORY, ABODE OF THE ST. LOUIS FUR COMPANY.

This out-of-proportion drawing of Fort Union is based on a cruder sketch by an unknown artist during the U.S. Army's occupation of the post, 1864-1865. *Courtesy Frank Leslie's Illustrated Newspaper, November 25, 1865.*

Then, on May 19, the season's first steamboat, the **Yellow Stone**, arrived. It brought replacements for Company I — Company B, 1st U.S. Volunteer Infantry Regiment. Company B was composed largely of captured Confederate soldiers who had agreed to serve on the frontier, rather than rot in prisoner-of-war camps. Their regiment was under the command of Colonel A. R. Dimon, all of twenty-three years old and wholly inexperienced. According to Chittenden, Fort Union was already acquainted with this regiment, seventeen of its members having deserted from Dimon's cruelty and walked all the way from Fort Pierre to Fort Union.[22]

On June 17, another steamboat arrived with the news that Pierre Chouteau, Jr., and Company had finally sold Fort Union. This news did not for the moment make any difference to Larpenteur. The fort's routine kept going. The 261 packs of robes and the elk skins had been shipped down the river. He watched the replacements practice skirmishing. In contrast to the last July 4, there were no celebrations this year "except two drahms given to the soldiers." He ordered new shelves for the retail store, where he used to clerk so long ago. Whitewashing took a lot of time. And soon it was time to build this year's hay rack.

On August 13, an overland express arrived ordering Company B to go down the river. They left immediately, leaving a lieutenant, a doctor, and eighteen soldiers to look after the government stores. To Larpenteur, "the Fort looks quite large and apparently desolate." A week later, a steamboat took even the detail away leaving only the lieutenant and one or two aides, and "leaving Larpenteur in charge of Fort Union, with Mr. Herrick Clerk, six working men, and Mr. Chas Conkle making in all ten men."[23]

Larpenteur set about putting the fort in order for the new owners. The Blackfoot annuities were stored "in the far end of the store," the pork and beef went into the root house, as did the salt. No less than 420 sacks of flour were stored in "the big ware house." He fenced in the area between the men's houses and the pickets and hung a door between the gable end of the men's houses and the Indian house, thus effectively boarding up the extreme western part of the fort where "the baggage [Army's?] is entirely locked up." He put the molasses "in one stall and boarded it up nailed the door, moved all the carpenter tools into the old carpenter shop, and swept up the fort good."

On September 17, the **Hattie May** brought "all of the honorable members of the N.W. Fur Co." Suddenly unemployed, Larpenteur boarded the steamboat and sailed away. The boat stopped at the site of Fort William, and Larpenteur took advantage of the delay to walk back to Fort Union to take care of some papers he had forgotten. When he got to the fort, where he had been the bourgeois, he found the gates locked. He went to a small cabin, where a man named Campbell lived, 100 yards distant, and took care of his business there. Larpenteur never explained his sudden departure from Fort Union, but his diary holds at least a trace of bitterness. But he would be back one day.[24]

Charles Chouteau, Pierre, Jr.'s son, had taken over the day-to-day operations of the company these past few years. By the end of 1864, he had pretty well decided to sell the Upper Missouri Outfit. Trade was off; the Sioux were still at war with the whites; and the Lincoln administration was suspicious of the company's activities and of the Chouteau family's loyalties.[25]

When in Washington in the spring of 1865, Charles met James Boyd Hubbell, in the freighting business in Minnesota. Chouteau suggested to Hubbell that the latter purchase the forts and their contents on the Missouri River. Hubbell promptly accepted the offer, "I made the purchase from Mr. Chouteau individually, but gave [Alpheus F.] Hawley, my partner ½ interest, he knew nothing of it." Later, J. A. Smith, Chicago; C. Francis Bates, New York; and J. A. Smith, Chicago; joined with Hubbell and Hawley to form the North Western Fur Company.[26]

In his reminiscences, Hubbell described the takeover of the forts on the upper Missouri. He said he was delayed in getting to Fort Union in 1865, because of the hostility of Col. Charles Dimon. One of the seventeen men of Dimon's regiment who had deserted and fled to Fort Union was an artist. It was this deserter, said Hubbell, who did the sketch of Fort Union that is customarily labeled "unknown soldier."

Illingworth and Bill 1866 photograph of a competing trading post near Fort Union. The establishment has been identified as belonging to the North Western Fur Company. That company, however, purchased Fort Union itself in 1865. These two log buildings more likely belonged to Gregory, Bruguier, and Geowey, who arrived at Fort Union in the spring of 1866 and purchased two buildings for $110. *Courtesy Montana Historical Society, Helena.*

Despite the decline in trade, the North Western Fur Co. apparently had a profitable first year at Fort Union. There being no other bidders, the company was able to acquire all the army stores in the fort for $2,000. Hubbell then had these supplies transported to Fort Benton and sold them to miners for about ten times their cost to him. It seems, too, that the winter of 1865-66 saw a fairly good trade in robes.[27]

In the spring of 1866, a competitor to Hubbell, apparently called "Gregory, Bruguier, and Geowey" appeared at Fort Union. From one Phillip Alourey they purchased a building "near the fort to be used for a store," for $100. Later, they purchased a second log house for $10. Little is known about these gentlemen except that they kept a fair stock of goods and sold to everyone who came their way. About the height of the Sioux troubles at Fort Union, in December 1866, Indian Agent Mahlon Wilkinson, staying at the fort, gave permission to the North Western Fur Company's bourgeois, Mr. Pease, to tear these structures down to prevent the Sioux from firing them. Their lumber was used for firewood inside the fort. Wilkinson promised to pay the competition for its loss.[28]

With the Civil War over, the U.S. Army turned its attention once

Fort Union

On the north bank of the Missouri 5 miles above the Yellowstone.
Looking up the river, N. W. May 27th 1866. G. S.

In 1866, Montana pioneer Granville Stuart made this sketch of Fort Union on one of his trips on the Upper Missouri. Although he exaggerated the size of the weathervanes on the bastions and added a non-existent third floor to the northeast (right) bastion, he nonetheless captured the fort's appearance in its decline.
Courtesy Montana Historical Society, Helena

again to the settlement of differences with the western tribes, particularly the Sioux. An inspecting officer arrived at Fort Union in 1866; his mission was to make a determination for a site for a permanent fort in the vicinity of the river junction. He agreed with General Sully and did not pick Fort Union, but chose the site at the junction. Shortly thereafter, on June 12, a company of the 13th U.S. Infantry under Captain W. G. Rankin arrived and commenced building Fort Buford.[29]

Granville Stuart, handy with a pen and sketch pad, stopped at Fort Union in May 1866; "We stopped awhile at this fort and got some ice at five cents per pound, and I took a slight sketch of it." It seemed to him that there were very few employees about, and the fort itself "had a sort of 'played out' look, and is evidently on the decline."[30]

Boller passed Fort Union for the third time that summer. To him, everything at Fort Union seemed the same, "and some few of the old retainers were still about." Farther down, he saw the soldiers building their new post.[31] By June 11, Larpenteur was back at Fort Union also.

Fort Union was no longer Larpenteur's responsibility, and his diary for the next few months sheds less light on the fort than usual. He did describe an amusing but potentially dangerous incident on July 4, a "rather dry day for Fort Union two shots were fired both pieces were turned up side down and one corner of the Fort damaged." It reached 102° that day and, before it was over, "we had one of the heavest thunder Storm[s] I ever heard at this place which took place at early bed time the flag staff was struck." Later in July, during the distribution of annuities, the fort was set on fire in the night. The Sioux were suspected since, "it had been started on the out Side." However, the fire was extinguished immediately.[32]

During the fall and winter of 1866-67, the Sioux harassed Fort Union and Fort Buford time after time. One of the more observant witnesses was a sutler at Fort Buford, Charles W. Hoffman, later a prominent banker in Bozeman, Montana. Hoffman spent much of his time up at Fort Union and witnessed many of its experiences. The first Sioux incident after his arrival occurred December 20, when a few of them attacked a man riding in a sleigh between the two forts. On New Year's Day Hoffman visited Fort Union under an escort of soldiers. On the way home, two men were following behind the escort when they were cut off by the Sioux less than one mile from Fort Buford. At least one soldier was killed in the rescue.

Two weeks later, Hoffman witnessed the Sioux chase two Assiniboin women at Fort Union out wooding. They killed one before being driven off by "a shot from one of the six pounders on the corner of the fort facing the river." On one occasion during the winter, Sitting Bull came to Fort Union from his camp some ten miles distant. He met with Bourgeois Pease outside the fort, and demanded and received a red shirt. Hoffman said the soldiers then were given the order to shoot red-shirted Indians.

Pease welcomed all the men he could get at Fort Union. Hoffman recalled that there were "about thirty white men and a lot of friendly Assinniboine Indians to help guard." To prevent a night attack, they built two large lanterns out of glazed window sash, moulding the candles in a piece of 2½-inch pipe. "We put them outside at the opposite corners from the bastions and kept them burning dark nights." Unfortunately, these do not appear in the one photograph of the exterior taken in 1866.

Fort Union from the north, 1866. Deterioration is becoming evident, particularly of the northeast (left) bastion. *Illingworth and Bill Photograph, Courtesy Montana Historical Society, Helena.*

As a sort of climax to this time of troubles, Hoffman described the arrival of Thundering Bull and "a large party of Santee and Cuthead Sioux." For some reason, Pease or Wilkinson decided to entertain Thundering Bull in the Indian house where he and his more important men spent their first night. The next day Pease, apparently feeling secure, sent a detachment of the fort's personnel out wooding.

Hoffman was in the (retail?) store talking to a friend when he noticed the Sioux, "in full paint and feathers," on their way to Pease's office. He said that Wilkinson at that moment was "up in the look-out over the mess houses." This possibly was a new structure located toward the north end of the fort so that it looked over the north gate.

Hoffman, armed, entered Pease's room where he found the bourgeois "seated near a window and a round table near him . . . . The Indians were seated on the floor," except Thundering Bull, who had taken a chair. Hoffman suggests that a rather tense meeting took place but, in the end, danger was averted when Pease told the Indians that powder had been distributed throughout the fort so that it could all be blown up, presumably including Thundering Bull. Despite the drama sensed by Hoffman, there remains the possibility that Thundering Bull's only intention was to carry out a trade.[33]

The North Western Fur Company kept Fort Union in operation throughout 1866 and into the next summer. By 1867, however, Hubbell decided to give up the post as an unprofitable operation. He hired the **Luella** sometime in this period to transport his goods up to Fort Benton.[34] He also opened a store at Fort Buford, which had increased in size to 500 soldiers. Charles Larpenteur, who, in the spring of 1867, had begun building an adobe trading store just outside Fort Union, decided that he too would open a store at Buford. He commenced a log building, 120 feet in length. For the moment the soldiers could choose from three traders: the military sutler, the North Western Fur Co., and Larpenteur.[35]

In June of 1867, General Sully, accompanied by Father DeSmet, arrived at Fort Buford in an effort to arrange a peace with the Sioux. On July 4, both men came up to Fort Union for a visit; otherwise the holiday passed quietly.

Larpenteur was still at his adobe store just outside Union when, on August 4, he witnessed the beginning of the end for the thirty-eight-year-old fort: "The Miner [a steamboat] arrived at Union, and left at about one oclock after having demolished the old Fort Union Kitchen for the Steamboat wood." On that same day, he wrote, "Fort Union is sold to the government to build up Fort Buford." On August 8, he wrote "The Soldiers Commenced tearing down the Fort Union yesterday." Apparently, Larpenteur himself had been living in Fort Union while his own establishment was being finished for he recorded on August 10 that he moved out of Fort Union. During these past few days, Larpenteur had had his own men hard at work building a bastion for his new establishment, apparently a little concerned that Fort Union would no longer offer any protection. On August 12, however, he made the decision to open a store at Fort Buford, and it was not long before this new project was taking most of his time.

On August 25, Larpenteur noted that "the pony express arrived from above." It appears, however, the express station was at Fort Buford rather than at his store. Referring to the disappearance of Fort Union, he wrote on August 26 that "the Carpenter tore down the Black Smith Shop and put his tools in order, to rebuild the Shop at Buford."

Through September, Larpenteur kept both stores in operation. Then he received a setback when the commanding officer at Buford forbade temporarily the soldiers from trading with him. This did not discourage him, and he continued to enlarge and improve upon his new establishment outside Buford. On October 14, he acquired "fourty logs from the old root house built by the government whilst quartered in Fort Union" in 1864. In November, Larpenteur had his men haul twenty-one loads of logs, three loads of slabs, and one of lumber from Fort Union. While he did not see fit to explain the circumstances, it seems likely that the Army and Hubbell had both taken what they needed out of the old fort and had left the rest for whomever had use for it.

Larpenteur and his men were now quartered in their new establishment and, on November 23, he wrote in his journal that his Union store had been abandoned.[36]

Five years after Larpenteur wrote that the U.S. Government bought Fort Union, the post surgeon, Washington Matthews, wrote that Union "was never owned by the Government nor, as far as I can learn, was any rent ever paid for it." Matthews was right that the Army did not pay rent for its use of the fort in 1864-65. Hubbell put in a claim for rent for that period (even though the post was owned by Pierre Chouteau, Jr. and Company for part of that time) but failed to obtain compensation.

According to Larpenteur, however, Hubbell did sell the materials of the post to the Army in 1867. Actually, Matthews agreed with Larpenteur by noting that these materials went into the construction of Fort Buford. It was not a proud ending for the grand old establishment that had for so long been the capital fort of the upper Missouri.

Dr. Matthews, in visiting the site around 1872, mentioned a cemetery "about one hundred paces east of the ruins of Union and separated from them by a little ravine." The little ravine is still there today, but all traces of a cemetery have long since disappeared. While Larpenteur never made clear just where he built his adobe store in 1867, Matthews described also "the ruined adobe walls to the west of the old fort." It all lay in ruins now; there was no proud fort.

Notes

1. U.S. Congress, House, Ex. Doc. No.56, "Reports of Explorations and Surveys, to Ascertain the most Practicable Route for a Railroad from the Missouri River to the Pacific Ocean, 1853-55,"36th Cong., 1st sess., vol.12, pp.70-71. Kennedy, p.216. The description of the party's arrival is from Robert Taft, **Artists and Illustrators of the Old West, 1850-1900** (New York: Charles Scribner's Sons, 1953), pp. 17-18. Taft believes the author of the description to have been Elwood Evans.

2. Taft, pp.8 and 20.

3. Lieutenant G. K. Warren, **Preliminary Report of Explorations in Nebraska and Dakota . . . 1855-'56-'57** (Washington: Government Printing Office, 1875), pp.15-16.

4. F. V. Hayden, **Contributions to the Ethnography and Philology of the Indian Tribes of the Missouri Valley** (Philadelphia: C. Sherman & Son, 1862), p.387: Gens du Gauche, 100 lodges; Gens du Lac, 60 lodges; Gens des Roches, 50 lodges; Gens des Filles, 60 lodges; Gens des Canots, 220 lodges; Gens du Nord, 30-50 lodges. Each lodge represented four persons.

5. Edwin Hatch Papers, Minnesota Historical Society, St. Paul. J. Cecil Alter, **Jim Bridger** (Norman: University of Oklahoma Press, 1962), p.262.

6. John C. Ewers, "Literate Fur Trader, Edwin Thompson Denig," **Montana Magazine of History** 4 (Spring 1954):1-9.

7. Kipp, January 29, 1857, to Chouteau, Folder 1858-59, Chouteau Coll., MoHS.

8. Larpenteur, **Forty Years**, 2:158-60.

9. James B. Musick, "Three Sketch Books of Carl Weimar [sic]," **Bulletin of the City Art Museum of St. Louis**, 27 (1942):10-14. William R. Hodges, **Carl Wimar, A Biography** (Galveston: Charles Reymershoffer, 1908), pp.11, 17, and 21-22. Taft, p.42. Carl Wimar Sketch Books and Sketches, MoHS.

10. Taft, pp.36-40.

11. U.S. Congress, Senate, Ex. Doc. No. 77, "Report of the Secretary of War . . . on the Exploration of the Yellowstone . . . report of Capt. William F. Raynolds, 1859 and 1860, 40th Cong., 1st sess., pp.114 and 145-47.

12. John Mason Brown, "A Trip to the Northwest in 1861," **The Filson History Quarterly** 24 (1950):128 and 219. The **Chippewa** exploded before reaching Fort Benton. Sister Dolorita Marie Daugherty, "A History of Fort Union (North Dakota), 1829-1867," (Ph.D. diss., St. Louis University, 1957), pp.154-56, describes Meldrum as a white man who was in the fur trade thirty-six years and eventually became a long hair. He died at Fort Union in 1865.

13. Taft, p.52. W. H. Schieffelin, "Crossing the Rockies in 61," **Recreation** 3 (1895):14-17. George Bird Grinnell, "Recollections of the Old West, Appreciation

of . . . William de la Montagne Cary," **The American Museum Journal** 17 (1917):333-34.

14. P. Chouteau & Co., February 6, 1861, to Chas. Primeau, Folder 1860-65, Chouteau Coll., MoHS.

15. James Harkness, "Diary of James Harkness, of the Firm of LaBarge, Harkness and Company," **Contributions to the Historical Society of Montana** 2 (1896):343-347.

16. Henry A. Boller, **Among the Indians, Eight Years in the Far West, 1858-1866** (Philadelphia: T. Ellwood Zell, 1868), pp.369-86.

17. Robert G. Athearn, **Forts of the Upper Missouri** (Englewood Cliffs, N.J.: Prentiss-Hall, 1967), p.89. Raymond L. Welty, "The Frontier Army on the Missouri River, 1860-1870," **North Dakota Historical Quarterly** 2 (1927-28):88-89.

18. Robert M. Utley, **Frontiersmen in Blue, The United States Army and the Indian, 1848-1865** (New York: Macmillan, 1967), pp.274-78. Robert H. Jones, **The Civil War in the Northwest** (Norman: University of Oklahoma Press, 1960), p.75. Joseph Mills Hanson, **The Conquest of the Missouri, Being the Story of the Life and Exploits of Captain Grant Marsh** (Chicago: A. C. McClure, 1909), pp.55-60. Athearn, pp.140-43.

19. Utley, p.279. Athearn, p.143. Although some accounts have the Wisconsin Volunteers arriving at Fort Union as early as April, Larpenteur's journal states clearly they arrived in June aboard the **Yellow Stone**.

20. "Iowa Troops in the Sully Campaign," **The Iowa Journal of History and Politics** 20 (1922):427. Overhold Papers, 1863-1864, Minnesota Historical Society.

21. Athearn, p.144. Douglas C. McMurtrie, "Pioneer Printing in North Dakota," **North Dakota Historical Quarterly** 6 (1931-32):222-26 and 222n. The first edition of the **Frontier Scout** complained about the awful smells at Fort Union and asked Larpenteur to improve the sanitation.

22. Hiram Martin Chittenden, **History of Early Steamboat Navigation on the Missouri River . . .** , 2 vols. (New York: Francis P. Harper, 1903), 2:264. D. Alexander Brown, **The Galvanized Yankee** (Urbana: University of Illinois Press, 1963), pp.73, 91, and 109.

23. The lieutenant and his men left on August 30.

24. Larpenteur, "Journal, 1864-1866," and **Forty Years**, 2:377.

25. Sunder, pp.260-62. Larpenteur, **Forty Years**, 2:366.

26. "Letters, Accounts, Legal Papers, Undated," Hubbell Papers, Minnesota Historical Society. The quotation was found written in the margin of Hubbell's personal copy of Chittenden, **Early Steamboating**, 1:239, and was signed "J. B. H." Most references to the company found in the Hubbell Papers called it the North Western Fur Company, or N. W. F. Co. Other names popularly assigned included the Northwestern Fur Co., Northwest Fur Co., and North West Fur Co. See Lucille M. Kane, "New Light on the Northwestern Fur Company," **Minnesota History** 34 (1955):325n.

27. **St. Louis Dispatch**, August 3, 1901, in folder, "Misc. Notes & Clippings"; and "Affidavits to Hubbell's Claim, 1900-1903," both in Hubbell Papers, Minnesota Historical Society.

28. "Misc. Notes & Clippings," Hubbell Papers; and Gregory, Bruguier, and Geowey Papers, both in Minnesota Historical Society.

29. Athearn, pp.226-27. Washington Matthews, "History of Fort Buford, Dakota Territory, and Locality," 1869, Montana Historical Society, Helena.

30. Granville Stuart, **Diary and Sketchbook of a Journey to 'America' in 1866 . . .** (Los Angeles: Dawson's Book Shop, 1963), p.34.

31. Boller, p.415.

32. Larpenteur, "Journal, 1864-1866." The old flagstaff had long since disappeared. The lightning struck a shorter staff mounted on a tower.

33. Affidavits re Claims, 1900-1903, Affidavit by Charles W. Hoffman, Hubbell Papers, Minnesota Historical Society. See also Athearn, pp.232-34.

34. Hanson, p.77.

35. Larpenteur, **Forty Years**, 2:388-89. Larpenteur was backed at this time by the firm of Durfee and Peck, St. Louis.

36. Larpenteur, "Journal, 1844-66."

Appendix

Chronology

1673.   Louis Jolliet and Jacques Marquette discovered the mouth of the Missouri River.

1805.   Meriwether Lewis and William Clark explored the junction of the Yellowstone and Missouri rivers, en route to the Pacific coast.

1808.   John Jacob Astor organized the American Fur Company.

1822.   Andrew Henry and William H. Ashley established a temporary trading post at the junction of the Missouri and Yellowstone rivers, called Fort Henry.

1822.   Columbia Fur Company formed. Kenneth McKenzie was its dominant personality.

1823.   Stone, Bostwick, and Co. became agent for the American Fur Company in St. Louis.

1823.   American Fur Company reorganized into Northern Department and Western Department, with Ramsay Crooks in charge of both.

1825.   Brigadier General Henry Atkinson set up a temporary camp, Camp Barbour, at the mouth of the Yellowstone River.

1825.   Ramsay Crooks married Bernard Pratte's daughter, Emilie.

1827.   Bernard Pratte and Company, St. Louis, assumed control of the Western Department, Pierre Chouteau, Jr., being the principal officer.

1827.   Columbia Fur Company joined the American Fur Company. Its name was changed to Upper Missouri Outfit, with McKenzie in charge.

1829.   Kenneth McKenzie founded Fort Union near the junction of the Missouri and Yellowstone.

1830.   Prince Paul, Duke of Württemberg, visited Fort Union.

1830.   The Assiniboin Chief, Tchatka or le Gaucher, failed in an attempt to attack Fort Union.

1831.   Steamboat **Yellow Stone** reached Fort Tecumseh on the Missouri.

1831.   McKenzie succeeded in beginning trade with the Blackfeet Indians. Fort McKenzie eventually established.

1832.	Fort Union partially destroyed by fire.
1832.	McKenzie established Fort Cass on the Yellowstone to trade with the Crow Indians.
1832.	Fort Tecumseh rebuilt and renamed Fort Pierre.
1832.	Steamboat **Yellow Stone** reached Fort Union. Artist George Catlin and Pierre Chouteau, Jr., on board.
1832.	Congress passed a bill prohibiting liquor in the Indian country.
1833.	Robert Campbell and William Sublette established Fort William at mouth of Yellowstone River.
1833.	Prince Maximilian of Wied and the artist Karl Bodmer visited Fort Union and other posts.
1833.	A wind storm blew down two sides of Fort Union's palisades in December.
1833.	McKenzie set up a distillery at Fort Union for the manufacture of alcohol.
1833.	Nathaniel Wyeth passed through Fort Union en route from his Pacific Northwest posts.
1833.	News of McKenzie's still reached the federal government. The American Fur Company almost lost its trading license.
1834.	McKenzie left Fort Union. He visited Prince Maximilian in Germany. James Archdale Hamilton and Daniel Lamont were acting bourgeois during McKenzie's absence.
1834.	John Jacob Astor retired from the fur trade. Pratte, Chouteau, and Co. bought out the Western Department; Ramsay Crooks took over the Northern Department.
1834.	Pratte, Chouteau, and Co. bought out Campbell and Sublette.
1835.	McKenzie returned to Fort Union in the fall.
1836.	Pratte, Chouteau, and Co. purchased Fort Laramie on the North Platte.
1837.	McKenzie retired from active duty in the fur trade. He lived in St. Louis.
1837.	Smallpox epidemic on the upper Missouri River.
1838.	Pratte, Chouteau, and Co. reorganized as Pierre Chouteau, Jr., and Co.
1840.	Father Pierre DeSmet, S. J., paid his first of many visits to Fort Union. James Kipp was the bourgeois.

1842.	Fox, Livingston, and Co. (also called the Union Fur Co.) established Fort Mortimer at the mouth of the Yellowstone.
1843.	John James Audubon and party visited Fort Union.
1844.	Kenneth McKenzie returned to Fort Union to resolve management problems. He remained on the upper Missouri until the spring of 1845.
1844.	Jim Bridger and a party of trappers spent the winter of 1844-45 at Fort Union.
1845.	The Union Fur Co. sold out to Pierre Chouteau, Jr., and Co.
1846.	Harvey, Primeau, and Co. established Fort William at the mouth of the Yellowstone.
1846.	War with Mexico.
1847.	The first notice of Sioux in the vicinity of Fort Union was made during the winter of 1847-48.
1847.	Tourist John Palliser spent the winter of 1847-48 at Fort Union. James Kipp was the bourgeois.
1848.	Edwin Thompson Denig was promoted to bourgeois of Fort Union.
1848.	Alexander Culbertson promoted to chief agent of the Upper Missouri Outfit.
1849.	Fort Laramie was sold to the U.S. Army.
1850.	Pierre Chouteau, Jr.'s, son, Charles, took over supervision of the company.
1851.	First notice of a white woman at Fort Union, Mrs. Joseph LaBarge.
1851.	Swiss artist Rudolph F. Kurz arrived at Fort Union, as a clerk. He returned home in 1852.
1853.	Isaac I. Stevens and his railroad surveying party arrived at Fort Union. Artist John Mix Stanley took the first daguerreotypes of the post.
1855.	Col. William S. Harney, 2d Dragoons, led a punitive expedition against the Sioux in Nebraska and on the Missouri River.
1856.	Lieutenant G.K. Warren and F. V. Hayden visited Fort Union while on a trip of exploration.
1856.	Sir George Gore and Jim Bridger stopped at Fort Union.
1856.	Edwin Denig retired from the fur trade. James Kipp again became bourgeois.

1856.	Another smallpox epidemic on the upper Missouri.
1856.	On December 1, 400 Sioux raided Fort Union.
1858.	Artist Carl Wimar from St. Louis visited Fort Union.
1860.	Artist William Jacob Hays visited Fort Union
1860.	Captain William F. Raynolds and Lieutenant Henry E. Maynadier, Yellowstone Expedition, arrived at Fort Union. They called their temporary camp, Camp Humphreys. Robert Meldrum was the bourgeois of the fort.
1860.	Gold was discovered in Idaho.
1861.	Artist William M. Cary and associates stopped at Fort Union.
1861.	Civil War began in the United States.
1861.	Sioux again raided Fort Union.
1862.	Sioux attacked settlements in Minnesota.
1863.	Henry A. Boller visited Fort Union.
1863.	Gold discovered in Montana.
1864.	In June, a company of infantrymen (Co. I, 30th Wisconsin Infantry) was stationed at Fort Union. Charles Larpenteur was now the bourgeois.
1864.	Sioux raided the fort's horse herd in July.
1864.	Brigadier General Alfred Sully led an army force against the Sioux. The troops reached Fort Union in August.
1864.	Montana Territory established.
1865.	In April, Sioux attacked three soldiers near the fort, killing one.
1865.	Company B, 1st U.S. Volunteer Infantry Regiment, replaced Company I in May.
1865.	In June, word arrived that Pierre Chouteau, Jr., and Co. had sold Fort Union to the North Western Fur Co. (James Boyd Hubbell and others). Frederick D. Pease became the bourgeois.
1865.	The army left Fort Union in August.
1866.	Competition in the form of Gregory, Bruguier, and Geowey appeared briefly at Fort Union.
1866.	Advance party of the Thirteenth Infantry, U.S. Army, arrived at the mouth of the Yellowstone on June 12 and commenced building Fort Buford.
1866.	Granville Stuart visited Fort Union. Charles W. Hoffman became sutler at Fort Buford.

1866.	Fall and winter of 1866-67, Sioux harassed Forts Union and Buford repeatedly. Sitting Bull visited the traders at Fort Union.
1867.	North Western Fur Co. abandoned Fort Union; Hubbell opened a trade store at Fort Buford.
1867.	Charles Larpenteur, working for Durfee and Peck, opened trade stores at both Forts Union and Buford.
1867.	U.S. government purchased Fort Union, dismantled it, and used the materials in constructing Fort Buford. Later, the site of Fort Union was included in the Fort Buford Military Reservation.
1966.	Fort Union Trading Post National Historic Site was established as a unit in the National Park System.

BIBLIOGRAPHY

1. Manuscript Material

Baker Library, Harvard Business School, Mass. The library has a collection on John Jacob Astor and the American Fur Company that was gathered by Kenneth W. Porter for his study of Astor. In general, the collection consists of letter books, miscellaneous letters, maps, and plans. It tends to be particularly strong on the subjects of Astoria and Green Bay.

Detroit Public Library, Mich. Available here, on photostats, are two large volumes of Ramsay Crooks's correspondence with John Jacob Astor concerning the fur trade.

Joslyn Art Museum, Omaha, Neb. At present, the museum has an extensive exhibit of the work of three Western artists, Catlin, Bodmer, and Miller, including a Bodmer sketch of Fort Union. Also made available for a brief scanning was that portion of Maximilian's work that dealt with Fort Union.

Kansas State Historical Society, Topeka. Selected items from the Records of the U.S. Superintendency of Indian Affairs, St. Louis, Clark Papers.

Library of the Boston Athenaeum, Mass. Manuscript of the Diary of Isaac Sprague, of his trip up the Missouri with Audubon, 1843.

Minnesota Historical Society, St. Paul. Of importance were the **Hubbell Papers**, covering the period after the American Fur Co. sold Fort Union; the **Edwin Hatch Papers**, which describe briefly an Indian agent's stay at Fort Union; the **Gregory, Bruguier, and Geowey Papers**, 1863-1877, the papers of competing traders in the mid-1860s; the **Overholt Papers**, on microfilm, the papers of a soldier at Fort Union; and the most valuable **"Journals" of Charles Larpenteur**, who kept detailed accounts of life at Fort Union in the 1830s and again in the 1860s.

Missouri Historical Society, St. Louis. The extensive holdings of this society were indispensable to this study. Of importance were the **Kenneth McKenzie Papers**, 1796-1858; the **Steamboat Collections**, 1832-1867; the **Indians Collection**, wherein is the important letter of Henry L. Ellsworth, Ft. Leavenworth, to E. Herring, Indian Commissioner, November 8, 1833; the **Carl Wimar Papers** and the Wimar sketchbooks and a collection of his sketches; various **Ledger Books** and **Account Books of the American Fur Company; the Culbertson Collection**, containing a history of Indians by Edwin T. Denig; **the Joseph A. Sire Log Books**, a steamboat captain, 1841-47; the **Andrew Drips Collection**, 1820-60; and, the largest of all, the **Chouteau Collections**, 1828-69, plus folders of undated material.

Montana Historical Society, Helena. In addition to photographs and sketches of Fort Union, the society has a manuscript by Dr. Washington Matthews, "History of Fort Buford, Dakota Territory, and Locality," 1869.

New York Historical Society. This society has a well-indexed, extensive collection of documents pertaining to the American Fur Company.

New York Public Library. Of use was a collection of photostats of John Jacob Astor's Papers.

Public Archives, Ottawa, Ontario. These magnificent archives contain a large collection of American Fur Co. Papers which, however, relate chiefly to the Michilimackinac area.

St. Louis University. Sister Dororita Marie Dougherty, C. S. J., "A History of Fort Union (North Dakota), 1829-1867," Ph.D. Dissertation, 1957, 219 pp.

2. Government Publications, U.S. and Canada.

Culbertson, Thaddeus A. **Journal of an Expedition to the Mauvaises Terres and the Upper Missouri in 1850.** Edited by John Francis McDermott. Smithsonian Institution, Bureau of American Ethnology, Bulletin 147. Washington: U.S. Government Printing Office, 1952.

Donaldson, Thomas. **The George Catlin Indian Gallery in the U.S. National Museum.**

Reprinted from the Smithsonian's **Report** for 1885. Washington: Government Printing Office, 1887.

Ewers, John C. "George Catlin, Painter of Indians and the West." **Annual Report . . . Smithsonian Institution, 1955.** Washington: U.S. Government Printing Office, 1956.

House Executive Documents, 36th Cong., 1st Sess., No.56. "Reports of Explorations and Surveys, to Ascertain the most Practicable and Economic Route for a Railroad from the Missouri River to the Pacific Ocean, 1853-5." Vol.12, Books 1 and 2. Washington: Thomas H. Ford, 1860.

Kurz, Rudolph Friederich. **Journal of Rudolph Friederich Kurz.** Translated by Myrtis Jarrell. Edited by J. N. B. Hewitt. Smithsonian Institution, Bureau of American Ethnology, Bulletin 115. Washington: U.S. Government Printing Office, 1937.

Murray, Alexander Hunter. **Journal of the Yukon, 1847-48.** Edited by L. J. Burpee. Publications of the Canadian Archives--No.4. Ottawa: Government Printing Office, 1910.

National Park Service. **A Proposed Fort Union Trading Post National Historic Site, North Dakota-Montana.**1962.

Senate Miscellaneous Document, 32nd Cong., Special Sess., 1851. "Fifth Annual Report of the Board of Regents of the Smithsonian Institution . . . 1850." Appendix IV. Thaddeus A. Culbertson's Journal of 1850.

Senate Executive Document, 35th Cong., 2nd Sess., No.46. "Reports of Explorations and Surveys to Ascertain the Most Practicable and Economical Route for a Railroad from the Mississippi River to the Pacific Ocean, 1853-5." Washington: William A. Harris, 1859.

Senate Executive Document, 40th Cong., 1st Sess., No.77. "Report of the Secretary of War . . . on the Exploration of the Yellowstone . . . report of Capt. William F. Raynolds, 1859 and 1860."

Warren, Lt. G. K. Preliminary Report of Explorations in Nebraska and Dakota . . . 1855-'56-'57. Engineer Department, United States Army: U.S. Government Printing Office, 1875.

3. Periodicals and Articles

"Ancient Landmarks." **Forest and Stream.** 70 (1908):131.

Barbeau, Marius. "Voyageur Songs of the Missouri." **Bulletin of the Missouri Historical Society** 10 (1954) 336-50.

Brooks, George R., ed. "The Private Journal of Robert Campbell" **The Bulletin, Missouri Historical Society** 20 (1963):3-24.

Brown, John Mason. "A Trip to the Northwest in 1861." **The Filson History Quarterly** 24 (1950):103-36 and 246-75.

Butscher, Louis C. "A Brief Biography of Prince Paul Wilhelm of Württemberg (1797-1860)." **New Mexico Historical Review** 17 (1942):181-93.

Butscher, Louis C., ed. "An Account of Adventure in the Great American Desert by His Royal Highness, Duke Paul Wilhelm von Württemberg." **New Mexico Historical Review** 17 (1942):193-216 and 294-344.

Butscher, Louis C., ed. "Account of an Adventures in the Great American Desert as Told by Mr. (Baldwin) Moellhausen. Companion to Prince Paul of Württemberg." **New Mexico Historical Review** 17 (1942):217-25.

Connolly, James B. "Father De Smet in North Dakota." **North Dakota History** 27 (1960):5-24.

Ewers, John C. "Literate Fur Trader, Edwin Thompson Denig." **Montana Magazine of History** 4 (1954):1-12.

Gallaher, Ruth A. "The Indian Agent in the United States Before 1850." **The Iowa Journal of History and Politics** 14 (1916):3-55 and 173-238.

Grinnell, George Bird. "Recollections of the Old West, Appreciation of the . . .Canvases . . .Painted by William de la Montague Cary." **The American Museum Journal** 17 (1917):332-40.

Guthrie, Chester L. and Leo L. Gerald. "Upper Missouri Agency: An Account of Indian Administration on the Frontier." **The Pacific Historical Review** 10 (1941):47-56.

Harkness, James. "Diary of James Harkness, of the Firm of La Barge, Harkness and Company." **Contributions to the Historical Society of Montana** 2 (1896):343-61.

"Iowa Troops in the Sully Campaigns." **The Iowa Journal of History and Politics** 20 (1922):364-443.

Kane, Lucile M. "New Light on the Northwestern Fur Company." **Minnesota History** 34 (1955):325-29.

Kimball, James P. "Fort Buford." **North Dakota Historical Quarterly** 4 (1929-30):73-77.

Mattison, Ray H. "Fort Union, Its Role in the Upper Missouri Fur Trade." **North Dakota History** 29 (1962):181-208.

Mattison, Ray H. "The Upper Missouri Fur Trade, Its Methods of Operation." **North Dakota History** 42 (1961):1-28.

Mattison, Ray H. "The Indian Frontier on the Upper Missouri to 1865." **Nebraska History** 39 (1958):241-66.

McMurtrie, Douglas C. "Pioneer Printing in North Dakota." **North Dakota Historical Quarterly** 6 (1931-32):221-30.

Missouri. "The Cover: 'The Fur Press in the Trading Post.'" **Missouri Historical Society** 4 (1949):125-26.

Musick, James B. "Three Sketch Books of Carl Weimar." **Bulletin of the City Art Museum of St. Louis** 27 (1942):10-14.

Porter, Kenneth W. "Negroes and the Fur Trade." **Minnesota History** 15 (1934):421-33.

Reid, Russell and Gannon, Clell G. eds. "Journal of the Atkinson-O'Fallon Expedition." **North Dakota Historical Quarterly** 4 (1929):5-56.

Schieffelin, W. H. "Crossing the Rockies in 61." **Recreation** 3 (1895):14-17.

Stevens, O. A. "Audubon's Journey Up the Missouri River, 1843." **North Dakota Historical Quarterly** 10 (1943):59-82.

Stevens, O. A. "Maximilian in North Dakota, 1833-34." **North Dakota History** 28 (1961):163-69.

Stuart, James. "Adventure on the Upper Missouri." **Contributions to the Historical Society of Montana** 1 (1876):80-89.

Welty, Raymond L. "The Frontier Army on the Missouri River, 1860-1870." **North Dakota Historical Quarterly** 2 (1927-28):85-99.

Wesley, Edgar B. "Some Official Aspects of the Fur Trade in the Northwest, 1815-1825." **North Dakota Historical Quarterly** 6 (1931-32):201-09.

Westbrook, Hariette Johnson. "The Chouteaus and Their Commercial Enterprises." **Chronicles of Oklahoma** 11 (1933):786-97 and 942-66. This latter, Part 2, has a somewhat different title: "The Chouteaus. Their Contributions to the History of the West."

Woolworth, Alan R., and Wood, W. Raymond. "Excavations at Kipp's Post," **North Dakota History** 29 (1962):237-52.

4. **Books and Pamphlets**

Abel, Annie Heloise. **Chardon's Journal at Fort Clark, 1834-1839.** Pierre, S. D.: State of South Dakota, 1932.

Alter, J. Cecil. **Jim Bridger.** Norman: University of Oklahoma Press, 1962.

Athearn, Robert G. **Forts of the Upper Missouri.** Englewood Cliffs, New Jersey: Prentice-Hall, 1967.

Audubon, Maria R. **Audubon and His Journals.** 2 vols. Notes by Elliott Coues. New York: Dover Publications, 1960.

Berry, Don. **A Majority of Scoundrels, An Informal History of the Rocky Mountain Fur Company.** New York: Harper & Brothers, 1961.

Boller, Henry A. **Among the Indians, Eight Years in the Far West,** 1858-1866. Philadelphia: T. Ellwood Zell, 1868.

Brown, D. Alexander. **The Galvanized Yankees.** Urbana: The University of Illinois Press, 1963.

Burdick, Usher L. **Tales from Buffalo Land, The Story of Fort Buford.** Baltimore: Wirth Brothers, 1940.

Bushnell, David I., Jr. **Ethnographical Material from North America in Swiss Collections.** Reprinted from **American Anthropologist** 10 (1908).

Catlin, George. **A Descriptive Catalogue of Catlin's Indian Gallery ... of the North American Indians ... Exhibiting at the Egyptian Hall, Piccadilly, London.** Bartholomew Close: C. Allard, 1840.

Catlin, George. **Letters and Notes on the ... North American Indians.** 2 vols. London: Tilt and Bogue, 1842.

Catlin, George. **North and South American Indians. Catalogue ... of Catlin's Indian Cartoons ... and 27 canvas paintings of Lasalle's Discoveries.** New York: Baker & Godwin, 1871.

Catlin, George. **North American Indians, Being Letters and Notes 1832-1839.** 2 vols. Philadelphia: Leary, Stuart & Co., 1913.

Chittenden, Hiram Martin. **History of Early Steamboat Navigation on the Missouri River, Life and Adventures of Joseph La Barge.** 2 vols New York: Francis P. Harper, 1903.

Chittenden, Hiram Martin. **The American Fur Trade of the Far West.** 2 vols. New York: Press of the Pioneers, 1935.

City Art Museum of St. Louis. **Charles Wimar, 1828-1862, Painter of the Indian Frontier.** St. Louis: City Art Museum, 1946.

Denig, Edwin Thompson. **Five Indian Tribes of the Upper Missouri.** Edited by John C. Ewers. Norman: University of Oklahoma Press, 1961.

DeSmet, Pierre Jean. **Life, Letters, and Travels ... 1801-1873.** 4 vols. Edited by H. M. Chittenden and A. T. Richardson. New York, 1905.

DeVoto, Bernard. **Across the Wide Missouri.** Boston: Houghton Mifflin, 1947.

Ewers, John C. **Artists of the Old West.** New York: Doubleday, 1965.

Goetzmann, William H. **Exploration and Empire, The Explorer and the Scientist in the Winning of the American West.** New York: Alfred A. Knopf, 1967.

Hafen, LeRoy R. **The Mountain Men and the Fur Trade of the Far West.** 10 vols. Glendale: The Arthur H. Clark Co., 1965-72.

Hanson, Joseph Mills. **The Conquest of the Missouri, Being the Story of the Life and Exploits of Captain Grant Marsh.** Chicago: A. C. McClurg & Co., 1909.

Hayden, F. V. **Contributions to the Ethnography and Philology of the Indian Tribes of the Missouri Valley.** Philadelphia: C. Sherman & Son, 1862.

Hodges, William Romaine. **Carl Wimar, A Biography.** Galveston: Charles Reymershoffer, 1908.

Hyde, William and Howard L. Conard, eds. **Encyclopedia of the History of St. Louis.** New York: Southern History Co., 1899.

Johnson, Allen, ed. **Dictionary of American Biography.** 20 vols. New York: Charles Scribner's Sons, 1943.

Jones, Robert Huhn. **The Civil War in the Northwest.** Norman: University of Oklahoma Press, 1960.

Kennedy, Michael S., ed. **The Red Man's West.** New York: Hastings House, 1965.

Kimball, Maria Brace. **A Soldier-Doctor of Our Army, James P. Kimball.** Boston: Houghton Mifflin, 1917.

Larpenteur, Charles. **Forty Years a Fur Trader on the Upper Missouri, The Personal Narrative of Charles Larpenteur, 1833-1872.** Edited by Elliott Coues. Minneapolis: Ross & Haines, 1962.

Lavender, David. **The Fist in the Wilderness.** New York: Doubleday, 1964.

Mattison, Ray H. **Fort Union, Its Role in the Upper Missouri Fur Trade.** Reprinted from **North Dakota History** 29 (1962).

McDermott, John Francis, ed. **Audubon in the West.** Norman: University of Oklahoma Press, 1965.

McDermott, John Francis, ed. **Up the Missouri With Audubon, The Journal of Edward Harris.** Norman: University of Oklahoma Press, 1951.

McFarling, Lloyd, ed. **Exploring the Northern Plains, 1804-1876.** Caldwell: Caxton Printers, 1955.

Morgan, Dale, and others. **Aspects of the Fur Trade, Selected Papers of the 1965 North American Fur Trade Conference.** St. Paul: Minnesota Historical Society, 1967.

Morgan, Dale L. and Harris, Eleanor Towles, eds. **The Rocky Mountain Journals of William Marshall Anderson, The West In 1834.** San Marino: The Huntington Library, 1967.

Morgan, Dale L., ed. **The West of William H. Ashley . . . 1822-1839.** Denver: Fred A. Rosenstock, 1964.

Palliser, John. **The Solitary Hunter, or, Sporting Adventures in the Prairies.** London: George Routledge, 1856.

Parton, James. **Life of John Jacob Astor.** New York: The American News Co., 1865.

Phillips, Paul Chrisler. **The Fur Trade.** 2 vols. Norman: University of Oklahoma Press, 1961.

Point, Nicholas, S. J. **Wilderness Kingdom, Indian Life in the Rocky Mountains: 1840-1847.** Translated by Joseph P. Donnelly, S. J. New York: Holt, Rinehart and Winston, 1967.

Porter, Kenneth Wiggins. **John Jacob Astor, Business Man.** 2 vols. New York: Russell & Russell, 1966.

Prucha, Francis Paul. **A Guide to the Military Posts of the United States, 1789-1895.** Madison: State Historical Society of Wisconsin, 1964.

Story of Fort Union and Its Traders. Williston, N. D.: The Elks Lodge, n. d.

Stuart, Granville. **Diary & Sketchbook of a Journey to 'America' in 1866 & Return Trip up the Missouri River to Fort Benton, Montana.** Los Angeles: Dawson's Book Shop, 1963.

Sunder, John E. **The Fur Trade on the Upper Missouri, 1840-1865.** Norman: University of Oklahoma Press, 1965.

Taft, Robert. **Artists and Illustrators of the Old West, 1850-1900.** New York: Charles Scribner's Sons, 1953.

Taylor, Joseph H. **Sketches of Frontier and Indian Life on the Upper Missouri and Great Plains.** Pottstown, PA: Joseph H. Taylor, 1889.

Thomas, Davis, and Ronnefeldt, Karin, eds. **People of the First Man, Life Among the Plains Indians in Their Final Days of Glory, The Firsthand Account of Prince Maximilian's Expedition Up the Missouri River, 1833-34.** New York: E. P. Dutton, 1976.

Thwaites, Reuben Gold, ed. **Early Western Travels, 1748-1846,** vols. 22-25 (vols. 22-24 being Maximilian's Travels in the Interior of North America, 1832-1834; and vol. 25 being Bodmer's drawings). Cleveland: The Arthur H. Clark Co., 1906.

Thwaites, Reuben Gold, ed. **Early Western Travels, 1748-1846,** vol. 27 (being DeSmet's Letters and Sketches, 1841-1842). Cleveland: The Arthur H. Clark Co., 1906.

Utley, Robert M. **Frontiersmen in Blue, The United States Army and the Indian, 1848-1865.** New York: Macmillan, 1967.

Young, F.G., ed. **Sources of the History of Oregon.** Eugene: University Press, 1899.

INDEX

Stanley, John Mix: 72-73, 99
Stevens, Isaac I: 71-73, 99
Stone, Bostwick, and Company: 2, 97
Stuart, Granville: 89-90, 100
St. Ange: 61
St. Louis: 1-5, 10, 15, 21-22, 31, 34, 44-46, 48,
    56n, 59, 61, 74-75, 78, 97-98, 100
St. Mary: 72
St. Peters: 46
Sublette, Milton: 36n
Sublette, William: 21-23, 30-32, 36n, 47, 98
Sully, Alfred: 81-83, 90, 92, 100
Sumpter, George: 47
Taft, Robert: 94n
Taos: iv
Tchatka: 16, 97
Tennyson, (?): 34
Thundering Bull: 92
Tilton, (?): 3
Union Fur Company: 47-48, 99
Upper Missouri Outfit (UMO): 4, 10-13n, 31,
    34, 45, 48, 69n, 74, 87, 97, 99
U.S. Army: iv, 84, 86, 89, 93, 99, 100
Vancouver Island: iv
Warren, G.K: 72-73, 99
Washington: iv
Washington D.C: 26, 30-31, 46, 74, 88
Well Come: 82
Western Department, AFC: 2-6, 34, 97-98
Western Department, HBC: iv
White Earth River: 9
Whitman, Marcus: 58
Wilkinson, Mahlon: 82, 89, 92
Wimar, Charles (Carl): 75-76, 100
Winegar, Robert: 83
Winnipeg, Lake: 1
Württemberg, Paul Wilhelm: 16, 34-35n, 97
Wyeth, Nathaniel: 30-31, 98
Yellowstone River: iii, 1, 9-13n, 17, 19, 21-22,
    47, 51, 53, 55, 68, 75-76, 80-81, 83, 97-100
Yellow Stone: 18-19, 24, 82, 86, 95n, 97-98
Yukon River: iii